Test Prep Series

2019 Edition

GRE®
Analytical Writing:
Solutions To The Real
Essay Topics

60 Solved Issue and Argument topics with strategies to be used as benchmark

Expert Strategies and simplified methods to produce focused responses

Scoring Guides for Issue and Argument tasks as per the revised GRE Guidelines

VIBRANT
PUBLISHERS

GRE® Analytical Writing:
Solutions to the Real Essay Topics - Book 1

ISBN-10: 1-949395-00-6
ISBN-13: 978-1-949395-00-6
Library of Congress Control Number: 2011917936

This publication is designed to provide accurate and authoritative information in regard to the subject matter covered. The Author has made every effort in the preparation of this book to ensure the accuracy of the information. However, information in this book is sold without warranty either expressed or implied. The Author or the Publisher will not be liable for any damages caused or alleged to be caused either directly or indirectly by this book.

Vibrant Publishers books are available at special quantity discount for sales promotions, or for use in corporate training programs. For more information please write to **bulkorders@vibrantpublishers.com**

Please email feedback / corrections (technical, grammatical or spelling) to **spellerrors@vibrantpublishers.com**

To access the complete catalogue of Vibrant Publishers, visit **www.vibrantpublishers.com**

Table of Contents

Dear Student,

Thank you for purchasing **GRE Analytical Writing: Solutions to the Real Essay Topics - Book 1**. We are committed to publishing books that are content-rich, concise and approachable enabling more students to read and make the fullest use of them. We hope this book provides the most enriching learning experience as you prepare for your **GRE** exam.

Should you have any questions or suggestions, feel free to email us at **reachus@vibrantpublishers.com**

Thanks again for your purchase. Good luck for your GRE!

− Vibrant Publishers Team

facebook.com/vibrantpublishers

GRE Books in Test Prep Series

**Verbal Insights on the
GRE General Test**
ISBN: 978-1-946383-36-5

**Analytical Writing Insights on the
revised GRE General Test**
ISBN: 978-1-946383-68-6

**GRE Analytical Writing: Solutions to the
Real Essay Topics - Book 1**
ISBN: 978-1-949395-00-6

**GRE Analytical Writing: Solutions to the
Real Essay Topics - Book 2**
ISBN: 978-1-949395-01-3

**GRE Quantitative Reasoning:
520 Practice Questions**
ISBN: 978-1-946383-88-4

**GRE Text Completion and Sentence
Equivalence Practice Questions**
ISBN: 978-1-946383-32-7

**GRE Reading Comprehension: Detailed
Solutions to 325 Questions**
ISBN: 978-1-946383-30-3

**GRE Master Word List: 1535 Words
for Verbal Mastery**
ISBN: 978-1-946383-41-9

GRE Word List: 491 Essential Words
ISBN: 978-1-946383-40-2

6 Practice Tests for the GRE
ISBN: 978-1-946383-34-1

GRE Words in Context: List 1
ISBN: 978-1-946383-42-6

GRE Words in Context: List 2
ISBN: 978-1-946383-43-3

**GRE Words in Context: Challenging
List**
ISBN: 978-1-946383-44-0

**Conquer the GRE: Stress Management
& A Perfect Study Plan**
ISBN: 978-1-479216-95-6

For the most updated list of books visit
www.vibrantpublishers.com

facebook.com/vibrantpublishers

Chapter 1

Introduction to the
Analytical Writing Measure

The Analytical Writing Measure is intended to assess your ability to think critically and write effectively about a topic while following specific directions. You will not need any specific content knowledge to complete either in this portion of the test. The purpose of both writing pieces is to determine your readiness to perform appropriately at the graduate level.

During this portion of the test, you will complete two writing tasks: Analyze an Issue and Analyze an Argument. For each portion, you will have 30 minutes to read the prompt and directions and to plan and execute your response.

The two tasks are opposite in their nature. During the Analyze an Issue task, you will write persuasively as you express your point of view on the selected topic, which may be in the form of an opinion, a recommendation, a claim and reason, or the presentation of two points of view. It is important to read the directions carefully to ensure that your response is addressing the prompt correctly and to enable you to receive the highest score.

During the Analyze an Argument task, you will evaluate an argument to determine the strength of the facts and assumptions that it presents. You may be asked to evaluate the evidence to determine if the assumptions are correct, formulate questions that will need to be answered before determining if the assumptions are correct, what further evidence is necessary before the argument can be declared correct, or what steps should be completed before accepting a recommended course of action. As in the Analyze an Issue task, in the Analyze an Argument task, reading and following the directions carefully is the best way to ensure that you receive a high score for your efforts.

This page is intentionally left blank

Chapter **2**

Analyze an Issue Task

As you complete this task, you will have an opportunity to express your point of view on an issue. Because it is essentially your opinion, there is no "correct" answer. You must, however, support your point of view with sufficient evidence to show the strength of your argument. You may agree completely with the statement about the issue, partially agree with it, or completely disagree with it. Be certain to stay on topic and follow the directions carefully.

For example, you might be presented with a statement similar to the following:

It is always best to look before you leap.

One interpretation of this statement is that one should consider potential consequences before taking any action. The directions may instruct you to write a response in which you discuss the extent to which you agree or disagree with the statement and explain your reasoning for the position you take. If you agree with the statement, you should recall examples from your reading, your studies, or your own experience that support your position. Think about Holden Caulfield's actions in The Catcher in the Rye. His impulsive decision to spend some time alone in New York City before going home after his expulsion from Pencey Prep had unsatisfactory consequences. You may have taken some action in your own life that you regretted afterwards. On the other hand, you may disagree with the statement. Early explorers like Christopher Columbus had little idea about what they would find as they set out in their relatively small sailing vessels. If they had thought only about the dangers of their ventures, the new world would have been discovered much later. You can also take a qualified approach by agreeing with the statement to some extent. Remember, the best approach to a given prompt is the one you can argue the best. The GRE essay readers are trained to evaluate a wide variety of approaches to the issue and evaluate them on their strengths and weaknesses and not on the opinion expressed.

The following is a comprehensive list of the instructions that can accompany the statements in the Analyze an Issue task.

a) Write a response in which you discuss the extent to which you agree or disagree with the statement and explain your reasoning for the position you take. In developing and supporting your position, you should consider ways in which the statement might or might not hold true and explain how these considerations shape your position.

b)   Write a response in which you discuss the extent to which you agree or disagree with the recommendation and explain your reasoning for the position you take. In developing and supporting your position, describe specific circumstances in which adopting the recommendation would or would not be advantageous and explain how these examples shape your position.

c)   Write a response in which you discuss the extent to which you agree or disagree with the claim. In developing and supporting your position, be sure to address the most compelling reasons and/or examples that could be used to challenge your position.

d)   Write a response in which you discuss which view more closely aligns with your own position and explain your reasoning for the position you take. In developing and supporting your position, you should address both of the views presented.

e)   Write a response in which you discuss the extent to which you agree or disagree with the claim and the reasons on which that claim is based.

f)   Write a response in which you discuss your views on the policy and explain your reasoning for the position you take. In developing and supporting your position, you should consider the possible consequences of implementing the policy and explain how these consequences shape your position.

You may have had some experience with writing persuasively in high school or college, but you do not need to worry about employing specific rhetorical devices to receive a high score. It is important to stay on topic, present your argument in a coherent and cohesive manner, and to acknowledge counterarguments to strengthen your own. You should also make every attempt to use correct grammar, mechanics, and a variety of sentence structures to improve the fluency of your essay. The scoring guide that follows is reprinted from the Practice Book for the GRE Revised General Test, developed by Educational Testing Service.

Scoring Guide

Score 6

In addressing the specific task directions, a 6 response presents a cogent, well-articulated analysis of the issue and conveys meaning skillfully.

A typical response in this category:

a)   articulates a clear and insightful position on the issue in accordance with the assigned task

b)   develops the position fully with compelling reasons and/or persuasive examples

c)   sustains a well-focused, well-organized analysis, connecting ideas logically

d)   conveys ideas fluently and precisely, using effective vocabulary and sentence variety

e)   demonstrates facility with the conventions of standard written English (i.e., grammar, usage and mechanics), but may have minor errors

Score 5

In addressing the specific task directions, a 5 response presents a generally thoughtful, well-developed analysis of the issue and conveys meaning clearly.

A typical response in this category:

   a)   presents a clear and well-considered position on the issue in accordance with the assigned task

   b)   develops the position with logically sound reasons and/or well-chosen examples

   c)   is focused and generally well organized, connecting ideas appropriately

   d)   conveys ideas clearly and well, using appropriate vocabulary and sentence variety

   e)   demonstrates facility with the conventions of standard written English but may have minor errors

Score 4

In addressing the specific task directions, a 4 response presents a competent analysis of the issue and conveys meaning with acceptable clarity.

A typical response in this category:

   a)   presents a clear position on the issue in accordance with the assigned task

   b)   develops the position with relevant reasons and/or examples

   c)   is adequately focused and organized

   d)   demonstrates sufficient control of language to express ideas with reasonable clarity

   e)   generally demonstrates control of the conventions of standard written English but may have some errors

Score 3

A three response demonstrates some competence in addressing the specific task directions, in analyzing the issue and in conveying meaning, but is obviously flawed.

A typical response in this category exhibits ONE OR MORE of the following characteristics:

   a)   is vague or limited in addressing the specific task directions and/or in presenting or developing a position on the issue

   b)   is weak in the use of relevant reasons or examples or relies largely on unsupported claims

   c)   is poorly focused and/or poorly organized

   d)   has problems in language and sentence structure that result in a lack of clarity

   e)   contains occasional major errors or frequent minor errors in grammar, usage or mechanics that can interfere with meaning

Score 2

A two response largely disregards the specific task directions and/or demonstrates serious weaknesses in analytical writing.

A typical response in this category exhibits ONE OR MORE of the following characteristics:

a) is unclear or seriously limited in addressing the specific task directions and/or in presenting or developing a position on the issue

b) provides few, if any, relevant reasons or examples in support of its claims

c) is unfocused and/or disorganized

d) has serious problems in language and sentence structure that frequently interfere with meaning

e) contains serious errors in grammar, usage or mechanics that frequently obscure meaning

Score 1

A one response demonstrates fundamental deficiencies in analytical writing.

A typical response in this category exhibits ONE OR MORE of the following characteristics:

a) provides little or no evidence of understanding the issue

b) provides little evidence of the ability to develop an organized response (i.e., is extremely disorganized and/or extremely brief)

c) has severe problems in language and sentence structure that persistently interfere with meaning

d) contains pervasive errors in grammar, usage or mechanics that result in incoherence

Score 0

A typical response in this category is off topic (i.e., provides no evidence of an attempt to respond to the assigned topic), is in a foreign language, merely copies the topic, consists of only keystroke characters or is illegible or nonverbal.

Chapter 3

Solved Issue Tasks with Strategies

General Strategies

a) Restate the issue in a way that makes sense to you.

b) You could also determine what question is being answered by the statement. Creating a question may help you determine your position on the issue. If someone were to ask you this question, would you say yes, no, or maybe?

c) Next, create a statement that expresses the opposing viewpoint, using language similar to that of the original statement.

d) Think about alternative viewpoints. Is there another way to look at this issue? Can you qualify the original recommendation in some way? How can you answer all or some of the questions that you generated earlier?

e) From here, you must decide which point of view to address in your essay. Before you decide, carefully consider the following questions. You will have addressed several of them in the exercises you will perform below.

    i.   What, precisely, is the central issue?

    ii.   What precisely are the instructions asking me to do?

    iii.   Do I agree with all or any part of the claim? Why or why not?

    iv.   Does the claim make certain assumptions? If so, are they reasonable?

    v.   Is the claim valid only under certain conditions? If so, what are they?

    vi.   Do I need to explain how I interpret certain terms or concepts used in the claim?

    vii. If I take a certain position on the issue, what reasons support my position?

viii.   What examples - either real or hypothetical - could I use to illustrate those reasons and advance my point of view? Which examples are most compelling?

f)   Once you have decided on a position to defend, consider the perspectives of others who might not agree with your position. Ask yourself:

i.   What reasons might someone use to refute or undermine my position?

ii.   How should I acknowledge or defend against those views in my essay?

The next step should be listing the main reasons and support for your position. Keep in mind that the GRE readers scoring your response are not looking for a "right" answer—in fact, as far as they are concerned, there is no correct position to take. Instead, the readers are evaluating the skill with which you address the specific instructions and articulate and develop an argument to support your evaluation of the issue.

Issue Task 1

> *In any field of endeavor, it is impossible to make a significant contribution without first being strongly influenced by past achievements in that field.*
>
> Write a response in which you discuss the extent to which you agree or disagree with the statement and explain your reasoning for the position you take. In developing and supporting your position, you should consider ways in which the statement might or might not hold true and explain how these considerations shape your position.

Strategies

You might begin by restating the issue. In this case the issue is a negative statement that includes the word impossible. Consider how the statement would look if you replaced impossible with the word, possible.

In other words:

The only way that it is possible to make a significant contribution in any field of endeavor is to first be strongly influenced by past achievements in that field.

Or

The only possible way to make a significant contribution in any field of endeavor is to first be strongly influenced by past achievements in that field.

You could also determine what question is being answered by the issue statement.

By what means is it possible to make a significant contribution in a field of endeavor?

The interrogatory form of the statement may help some writers develop alternative viewpoints. The original issue statement is only one of several possible answers to the question.

Now think about the parts of the statement that provide evidence that you can affirm or refute.

   a) **the only possible way** – Is there no other way to make a significant contribution? Is nothing really original? Is everything derivative?

   b) **any field of endeavor** – Are there fields of endeavor that can be excluded from this statement? Can we even imagine fields of endeavor that might arise in the future?

   c) **strongly influenced** – Is it possible to be mildly influenced or tangentially influenced by past achievements?

   d) **contribution** – What kind of contribution? Is it a new invention? An idea? A procedure?

Next, create a statement that expresses the opposing viewpoint, using language similar to that of the original issue statement.

Opposing viewpoint:

In any field of endeavor, it is possible to make a significant contribution without being strongly influenced by past achievements in that field.

Or

Being strongly influenced by past achievements in any field of endeavor is not the only way to make a significant contribution to that field.

Identify the parts of the opposing statement that provide evidence to refute or affirm. Some of these may look very similar to those in the list generated above.

a) **contribution** – How does one determine the significance of any contribution? Significance may be subjective.

b) **any field of endeavor –** Are there fields of endeavor that can be excluded from this statement?

c) **influence** – What form of influence? Is it a product? An idea? A procedure?

d) **not the only way** – How might one contribute significantly without being influenced by past achievements?

Alternatives:

Is there any other way to look at this issue? By what means other than strong influence from past achievements can someone make a contribution to a field of endeavor? Begin by listing important fields of human endeavor: medicine, science, art, philosophy, literature, flight, etc. Think about experiences you have had, books you have read, course you have taken and come up with some examples of contributions to that field.

a) **Medicine** – Fleming and penicillin

b) Native Americans and willow bark

c) **Science** – Galileo and heliocentrism

d) **Art** – Picasso and cubism

e) **Literature** – Ezra Pound and imagism

f) **Energy** – prehistoric man and fire

What statements can you make about the items in your list? Fleming's, Galileo's, and prehistoric man's contributions came in the form of discovery. Picasso's and Pound's contributions came in the form of rejecting the previous achievements in their fields of endeavor. Galileo's discovery occurred also as he rejected the church's theory of the Earth as the center of the universe. Now you have two specific means of contribution: discovery of something new and rejection of something old.

Create a statement that expresses a viewpoint using the new ideas that you have uncovered.

New Viewpoint:

It is possible to make a significant contribution in any field of endeavor by rejecting past achievements in that field.

Or

All significant contributions in any field of endeavor occur as a result of an important discovery.

What evidence exists in these statements that provide points to support or refute?

a) **rejecting past achievements** – Is it possible to transform rather than reform an existing idea or product?

b) **discovery comes before achievement** – Every field of endeavor arises from an important discovery.

Now you must decide which point of view to address in your essay. Completing the prewriting activities has given you several choices and ideas for defending any of those choices. Even the viewpoints that are opposite of yours will have points that you can use in writing your response. As you review your notes, decide which of your ideas offer the strongest support for your position; you do not have to use all of them. Keep in mind that others may disagree with your position, so address their concerns in your response. Before you decide, carefully consider the following checklist. You will have addressed several of them in the exercises you have completed above.

a) I have identified the central issue.

b) I understand the instructions.

c) I have decided that I agree/disagree/partially agree with the issue and why.

d) I have identified the assumptions in the claim and determined whether or not they are reasonable.

e) If necessary, I can explain how I interpret any or all of the concepts and terms used in the claim.

f) I have identified my reasons for the position I have taken.

g) I have compelling examples to support my position.

The next step should be listing the main reasons and support for your position. You may use any of the above prewriting activities as you prepare evidence for supporting you point of view. Remember that the GRE readers scoring your response are not looking for a "right" answer. The readers are evaluating your ability to address the specific instructions and articulate and develop an argument to support your understanding and evaluation of the issue.

Position:

All significant contributions in any field of endeavor occur as a result of an important discovery.

Examples:

a) **Fire** – Once man learned to control it, he developed uses for it and sources of fuel to feed it.

b) **Medicine** – Man discovered that leaves, roots, and bark of trees and plants ameliorated pain and relieved the symptoms of other maladies

c) **Water power** – Man could harness the power of flowing water to turn wheels to grind grains and seeds.

Your notes do not have to be exhaustive. As you begin to write your essay, your brain will generate new ideas. Make certain that you keep the directions in mind as you develop your ideas. Use as many or as few paragraphs as you consider appropriate for your argument, but you should create a new paragraph when you move on to a new idea or example in support of your position. The GRE readers are not looking for a specific number of ideas or paragraphs. Instead, they are reading to determine the level of understanding of the topic and the complexity with which you respond.

In this task, you are asked to discuss the extent to which you agree or disagree with the statement. You may completely agree or disagree with the statement, or you may agree under certain conditions. You are also instructed to explain your reasoning and consider ways in which the statement might or might not hold true and explain how these considerations shape your position.

You may use any organizational strategy or form of reasoning to present your position as clearly and succinctly as possible. You may recall writing strategies that you learned in high school or a writing-intensive course that you took in college, but it is not necessary to employ any of those strategies. It is important that your ideas follow a logical progression and display strong critical thinking.

Sample Essay

The premise that significant contributions in any field can only be made through the influence from past achievements in that field holds true in the modern world. Modern appliances, advanced medicine, and improved fuel efficiency are founded on earlier models. The next big thing is simply a version of the last big thing. It may be thinner, smaller, faster, or more intuitive, but, fundamentally, it is the same thing. The ubiquitous television sets in people's homes today are probably hanging on the wall and have plasma or LCD screens. These bigger, brighter versions essentially perform the same function as the older, bulkier vacuum tube models; they bring moving pictures into our homes. The Band-Aids found in every medicine chest come in a variety of sizes, colors, with or without an antibacterial cream embedded, and even in liquid form. These superior bandages also perform the same function as their predecessors; they cover cuts and scrapes. In actuality, everything new is not very original. They are adaptations.

One must turn to the ancient world to recognize that the greatest contributions in any field of endeavor have come through discovery rather than invention or advancement. Early man discovered fire and realized he could use it to cook his food, warm his cave, and keep predators at bay. Eventually, he learned how to create it, preserve it, and carry it with him as he migrated to better hunting grounds or more temperate climates. Modern man has witnessed the harnessing of fire to create steam that powered ships and locomotives. It still heats our homes and cooks our food, but it also takes us into outer space.

At some point ancient man realized that round objects move more effectively over the ground than do square or rectangular objects, that the power of water could help man to accomplish tasks more easily, and that the leaves, roots, and bark of plants and trees provided relief from pain and other maladies. Thus, we have the wheel, grist mills on local streams, and aspirin in tablet form. Were it not for Franklin's flying a kite during a thunder storm or Fleming's discovery of penicillin, we would live in the dark and die from bacterial infections. When bold seafarers from Scandinavia and Western Europe sailed east and failed to fall off the edge of the earth, they discovered the fishing banks off the coast of Newfoundland and treasures in Mexico and opened the doors to modern-day travel.

In the final analysis, it is appropriate to assert that no one can contribute significantly in any field of endeavor without first being influenced by past achievements in that field. While those contributions generally improve the quality of our lives, it is likely that the next important discovery will have a profound effect.

Issue Task 2

> *Formal education tends to restrain our minds and spirits rather than set them free.*
>
> Write a response in which you discuss the extent to which you agree or disagree with the statement and explain your reasoning for the position you take. In developing and supporting your position, you should consider ways in which the statement might or might not hold true and explain how these considerations shape your position.

Strategies

Restate the issue. In this case, the issue is stated in the positive. It tells what formal education does. What does formal education not do?

In other words:

Formal does not set our minds and spirits free.

You could also determine what question is being answered by the issue statement.

What effect does formal education have on our minds and spirits?

Making the statement an interrogatory may clarify the issue. The original issue statement is only one of several possible answers to the question.

Now think about the parts of the statement that provide evidence that you can affirm or refute.

   a) **formal** – Formal simply means that it has a form. Would students, even outside the formal educational setting, develop or create a form for studying what they choose? Is some form necessary or inevitable?

   b) **restrain** – Does formal education hold back our minds and spirits?

   c) **tends** – Tends is not a strong word. Does this weaken the issue statement?

Next, create a statement that expresses the opposing viewpoint, using language similar to that of the original issue statement.

Opposing viewpoint:

Formal education tends to unleash our minds and spirits.

Identify the parts of the opposing statement that provide evidence to affirm or refute.

   a) **unleashes** – removes restraints or sets free

Alternatives:

Is there any other way to look at this issue? Can you qualify the original issue statement in some way? Perhaps a combination of structure and freedom is the best way to educate our citizens.

New viewpoint:

A formal structure combined with the choice to select areas of study is the most effective way to set our minds and spirits free.

Identify the parts of the new statement that provide evidence to affirm or refute.

a) **combination** – Does a combination dilute the effectiveness of one or both of the components?

b) **choice** – At what level of formal education are students competent to choose their course of study?

Now you must decide which point of view to address in your essay. Completing the prewriting activities has given you several choices and ideas for defending any of those choices. Even the viewpoints that are opposite of yours will have points that you can use in writing your response. As you review your notes, decide which of your ideas offer the strongest support for your position; you do not have to use all of them. Keep in mind that others may disagree with your position, so address their concerns in your response. Before you decide, carefully consider the following checklist. You will have addressed several of them in the exercises you have completed above.

a) I have identified the central issue.

b) I understand the instructions.

c) I have decided that I agree/disagree/partially agree with the issue and why.

d) I have identified the assumptions in the claim and determined whether or not they are reasonable.

e) If necessary, I can explain how I interpret any or all of the concepts and terms used in the claim.

f) I have identified my reasons for the position I have taken.

g) I have compelling examples to support my position.

The next step should be listing the main reasons and support for your position. You may use any of the above prewriting activities as you prepare evidence for supporting you point of view. Remember that the GRE readers scoring your response are not looking for a "right" answer. The readers are evaluating your ability to address the specific instructions and articulate and develop an argument to support your understanding and evaluation of the issue.

Position:

Formal education is the most effective means for introducing students to a wide variety of subjects in order for them to discover what sets their minds and spirits free.

Examples and reasons:

a) **variety** – formal education in America is comprised of content from various disciplines. Students will be exposed to grammar, writing, literature, science, math, foreign language, art, music

b) **discover** – exposure to a variety of disciplines provides opportunities to be inspired by a topic that students might never have found on their own

c) **most effective** – most is a qualifier – not saying it's the only means, just the best – other types of education may work better for some students

d) **introducing** – from primary grades through the first two years of most colleges, students are introduced to a variety of subjects – no major focus is determined, generally, until the end of the second year in college

Your notes do not have to be exhaustive. As you begin to write your essay, your brain will generate new ideas. Make certain that you keep the directions in mind as you develop your ideas. Use as many or as few paragraphs as you consider appropriate for your argument, but you should create a new paragraph when you move on to a new idea or example of support for your position. The GRE readers are not looking for a specific number of ideas or paragraphs. Instead, they are reading to determine the level of understanding of the topic and the complexity with which you respond.

In this task, you are asked to discuss the extent to which you agree or disagree with the statement. You may completely agree or disagree with the statement, or you may agree under certain conditions. You are also instructed to explain your reasoning and consider ways in which the statement might or might not hold true and explain how these considerations shape your position.

You may use any organizational strategy or form of reasoning to present your position as clearly and succinctly as possible. You may recall writing strategies that you learned in high school or a writing–intensive course that you took in college, but it is not necessary to employ any of those strategies. It is important that your ideas follow a logical progression and display strong critical thinking.

Sample Essay

In the book of Genesis in the bible, the story of creation reveals that God saw the world as void and having no form, so he took it upon Himself to give it form. He divided the land from the sea, populated his new world with animals and plants of every kind, separated the night from the day, and, finally, created man. Even God recognized the need for form. Without form there is void. Formal education is, at its most basic level, education that has some structure applied to it. Without structure in education, there is void.

Some might argue that formal education is too restrictive; the prescribed curriculum in most schools inhibits creativity and free thinking; and the pedagogy confines the imaginations of students. Some find a syllabus to be onerous, an anthology to be limiting, and a bell schedule to be jarring. Within this structured environment, however, is the opportunity to sample courses in Shakespeare, poetry, philosophy, geography, American history, sociology, French, Spanish, biology, physics, algebra, statistics, art, music, and physical education. This smorgasbord of academic offerings will surely contain something to tempt the palate of even the fussiest scholar.

Others may point to the structure or formality that exists outside of the world of education as a justification to similarly define academia. Upon leaving one's education behind, the former student will need to follow the structure imposed upon the world of work. The discipline to do so will have been developed during the years of formal education.

Left to his own devices, a child can indulge his whims by studying whatever interests him. Rarely does a child have the discipline to sustain that interest. He will move on to the next fleeting attraction. A variety of factors may influence his exposure to the world: his parents' educational level, family income, geographical location, and availability of arts and cultural performances. Through formal education these differences need not matter. Every child will get the same opportunities to read absorbing books, construct and perform scientific experiments, attend school assemblies, and connect to the Internet. Without the form of public education, there will likely be a void in this child's experience of the world.

Issue Task 3

> *In any field of inquiry, the beginner is more likely than the expert to make important contributions.*
>
> Write a response in which you discuss the extent to which you agree or disagree with the statement and explain your reasoning for the position you take. In developing and supporting your position, you should consider ways in which the statement might or might not hold true and explain how these considerations shape your position.

Strategies

A good starting point is to break down the statement and identify the assumptions it makes. Look for ambiguous phrasing and consider all possible exceptions – they represent weak points that you can defend or attack depending on your chosen position.

Statement breakdown

a) **Any field** – is it applicable to all fields? How about highly complex ones that require specialized knowledge?

b) **Beginner** – how do you classify the beginner? Based on age? Experience? Knowledge?

c) **More likely** – does it refer to statistical probability (numbers game)? Does it refer to inherent qualities of the beginner?

d) **Important contributions** – what constitutes an important contribution? What is the classification criterion: applicability, usefulness, impact?

Assumptions

a) Beginners are more likely to contribute, since there are more beginners than experts

b) Important contributions are not based on experience

c) Beginners have more creative minds, while experts are set in their ways

Pros and Cons

Pros

👍 Thinking outside the box (integrating and reorganizing existing understandings – a process essential to beginners

👍 With age, cognitive abilities deteriorate, it becomes harder to process new information (experts are often older)

👍 Beginners are determined – they have something to prove

👍 Beginners are freer to experiment – experts are set in their ways

👍 There are greater numbers of beginners, so a larger chance to bring accidental contributions

👍 Beginners have more willingness to try or evaluate new paths

👍 Beginners have more time (experts are committed to multiple projects and often have to perform supervisory roles)

👍 Beginners have less to lose by pursuing risky avenues

Cons

👎 Beginners that make important contributions are considered experts

👎 The aging brain is similar to the creative brain (based on neural imaging) – low inhibitions, high scores on crystallized IQ

👎 Experts are more productive, have a better work ethic

👎 Some fields are very complex (entry level knowledge is insufficient to provide deep insight)

👎 For beginners, lack of practical application can lead to correct but irrelevant insight (researching avenues that lead to nowhere

👎 Focused research (knowing the field allows you to conduct a targeted research)

👎 Historically, most of the great inventions come from experts between the ages of 30 to 50

👎 Experts have more freedom of choice when it comes to the research topic (beginners are limited by supervisors

👎 Experts can get more funding, or obtain it easier than beginners can (reputation)

👎 Experts enjoy more credibility

Examples:

a) Inventors and scientific contributors from the past

b) Studies linking age and creativity

c) Problem solving skills and methods (you can pair them up with the group that fits best)

d) Current research practices

Sample Essay

Humans have conquered their surroundings and overcome their limits in leaps and bounds marked by great innovations. Our ability to integrate and reorganize existing understandings, to bring new order to chaos, has been the driving force of our progress. It is no wonder that people seek to understand the process of innovation and encourage those that are most likely to succeed in revolutionizing the world.

So far, invention has been considered the patrimony of experts, and one of the reasons is the fact that, in order to be able to combine fragments of knowledge in new ways, one needs to have sufficient knowledge in the first place.

It is not difficult to understand why such perceptions abound, especially if we consider highly complex fields that require specialized, in depth, knowledge. Take for instance astrophysics or microbiology – a beginner in these fields would only possess summary knowledge of the forces at play and the processes involved. They wouldn't be able to revolutionize theories on dark matter without a basic understanding of quantum theories, and by the time they would have acquired this knowledge, they would be considered experts. This is also the case of Albert Einstein, whose major contributions in the field came as a steady progression after getting his PhD. Most important of all, Einstein's theory of relativity only started taking shape after years of teaching theoretical physics at the universities in Zurich and Prague, and two years spent studying continuum mechanics, the molecular theory of heat, and the problem of gravitation.

When it comes to establishing whether beginners or experts are more likely to revolutionize a new field, it is important to note that a lot of the past inventions have come from people that had to constantly struggle with a specific problem. A lot of the people that have contributed to the advancement of society were experts in a field (they were in the proper circumstances to encounter the problem and possessed sufficient knowledge to recognize and solve the issue at hand). This is the case of prominent physician, John Snow, whose field work in tracing the 1854 cholera outbreak in London is regarded as the founding event of epidemiology. He encountered many cases of viral diseases as a physician, which, alongside his skepticism of the then dominant miasma theory of infection, spurred him on to research the Soho epidemic and discover the source of the outbreak.

Moreover, one should always keep in mind that it's not sufficient to have a good idea; a researcher should also be able to support it and make it known. This holds especially true when considering the basic conditions for any form of research to be considered a major contribution in a field. Namely, said research should revolutionize its field of study, it should be known by other experts in the discipline and obtain external validation (even if at a later point in time). In this sense, experts enjoy more credibility than beginners, and are likely to be taken more seriously. Furthermore, experts already have networks in place and get quicker access to information like interesting research proposals and latest advancements. Companies and other researchers will choose to go to the person with a better reputation. The same can be said in terms of funding, experts can attract more funds for promising research– simply because they have more experience and an established reputation.

Studies have shown that experts are more productive and have better work ethic and time management skills. In addition, being an expert doesn't signify the death of creativity, like the statement implies, blindly sticking to one method has more to do with personality. The same goes for linking expertise with age, as neural imaging studies have shown that the aging brain is more creative, uninhibited and shows better crystallized IQ. Benjamin Jones has also found that over the past 100 years, the major scientific discoveries have come from people with ages between 30 and 50.

Overall, when it comes to having major contributions in a field, experts possess the advantage. They have more knowledge, an increased ability to organize the information they posses, more resources to fund research and a better work ethic than beginners.

Issue Task 4

> *The surest indicator of a great nation is represented not by the achievements of its rulers, artists, or scientists, but by the general welfare of its people.*
>
> Write a response in which you discuss the extent to which you agree or disagree with the statement and explain your reasoning for the position you take. In developing and supporting your position, you should consider ways in which the statement might or might not hold true and explain how these considerations shape your position.

NOTE: The above topic has wording similar to Issue Task 27 of GRE Analytical Writing Solutions to the Real Essay Topics - Book 1. However, if you read carefully you will notice that the task instructions are different. Hence, it is very important to read the topic as well as its instructions completely before you start to write your response.

Strategies

Statement breakdown

a) **Surest indicator** – Welfare is not the only indicator of greatness; it is not a causality relationship – welfare doesn't cause greatness, but can be used to measure it

b) **Great nation** – what constitutes a great nation? How do you define it? In terms of power, size, economy etc.?

c) **Rulers, artists or scientists** – categories of people whose contributions can be significant – are they the only ones with memorable achievements? What about athletes, spiritual leaders, military heroes, brilliant businessmen and other people that brought significant advancements in their fields?

d) **General welfare** – what is the degree of welfare? Meeting the basic needs of the people? What indicators do you use to measure it – safety, buying power etc.?

Assumptions

a) Great nations have a high level of welfare

b) The welfare of the people is more important than the achievements of rulers, artists and scientists

c) Rulers, artists and scientists are the only ones with notable contributions

Pros and Cons

Pros

- 👍 High living standards are a hallmark of civilized society

- 👍 Rulers, artists and scientists are not the only ones whose achievements contribute to a country's greatness

- 👍 Welfare is an indicator – something that when measured can tell the state of a country – it's economical and cultural prosperity

👍 Welfare encourages scientific development – in the sense that if people's basic needs are met, that gives them the freedom to pursue their vocations/ideals

👍 More programs and support systems for artists and scientists (scholarships, research funding etc.)

👍 Happiness studies are directly linked with productivity/ creativity

👍 People centered modern day philosophy – human resources are the most valuable

👍 Great thinkers (scientists) and artists are great in themselves, regardless of the nation they came from – their contributions transcend boundaries

Cons

👎 Historically speaking, countries are memorable due to the achievements of their rulers, artists and scientists

👎 Great rulers make welfare possible – they promote policies that support good living conditions for the citizens of the state

👎 Scientific advancements make life easier, increase the living standards

👎 Greatness is measured in contributions to world benefit – ruling principles like democracy, freedom of speech etc.

👎 Good rulers and scientific advancements drive the economy. Strong economies are indicative of great nations.

👎 A country's power is an indicative of greatness, and a major contributing factor in scientific advancements

👎 Cultural ideals help shape not only a nation, but the entire world

Examples:

a) Civilizations of the past, to showcase what history considers being great nations

b) Current great nations

c) Economical theories on welfare

d) Great achievements in the fields of science, great artists and commanders

Sample Essay

Current society, as a whole, has become highly invested in people centric policies – from governments that ensure the welfare of the citizens, to companies that place customer and employee values at their core. This transformation is in the spirit of Mahatma Gandhi's teachings, that "man becomes great exactly in the degree in which he works for the welfare of his fellow-men."

Throughout the ages, welfare has been an indicator of a nations' economical and cultural prosperity. High living standards point to economical stability, growth, abundance of resources – all of which are necessary to ensure that the populations' necessities are met. Moreover, the presence of welfare signals the existence of a cultural system capable of fostering the ideas necessary to support it. High living standards and civilization have always been linked – take for instance the great nations of the past, like Ancient Greece or Rome, hallmarks of civilization that have left a deep imprint on the world. In both of these cases, the quality of life of the average citizen was well above that of the people living in the neighboring countries – they had the buying power and the possibility to enjoy a wider variety of products and leisurely activities, while being less concerned with day to day survival.

In this sense, it can be said that welfare encourages creativity, by meeting people's basic needs which in turn gives them the freedom to pursue their vocations/ideals. Maslow's hierarchy of needs supports this idea. Maslow's theory states that an individuals' fundamental needs have to be fulfilled before he can focus on the higher level needs. What this means is that, for instance, metabolic requirements will tend to supersede self-actualizing actions, namely, artistic or creative activities will have to take a backseat to hunger or thirst. Countries where people's basic needs are being taken care of can afford to dedicate more time and resources to higher pursuits.

Moreover, countries with a high standard of living have the means to create programs and support systems for artists and scientists. The countries in northern Europe that is famous for the quality of life of the average citizen, have significant government support when it comes to education. Their tuition fees are much lower than in the USA, and they invest a greater deal of resources into scholarships and research funding than countries like India. More than that, the northern European countries strive to ensure not just the physical welfare of their citizens, but also their mental and ideological wellbeing by providing an open-minded climate where diversity can thrive. As Plato postulated in the Republic, the stability and success of a political community depends on the moral character of the people who make up that community.

From these arguments, it becomes apparent that rulers, artists and scientists are not the only ones whose achievements contribute to a country's greatness. But rather, economical power, one of the main characteristics of a strong nation, is dependent on the consumers and their buying power.

Ultimately, when assessing a nation's greatness, it all comes down to what traits best represent it. From what we have seen so far, the welfare of a nation's citizens, closely tied to their economic power, provides a nurturing environment for talents that will end up shaping the rest of the world and contributing to the benefit of mankind. As such, it can be said that general welfare is one of the surest indicators of a country's greatness.

Issue Task 5

> *As we acquire more knowledge, things do not become more comprehensible, but more complex and mysterious.*
>
> Write a response in which you discuss the extent to which you agree or disagree with the statement and explain your reasoning for the position you take. In developing and supporting your position, you should consider ways in which the statement might or might not hold true and explain how these considerations shape your position.

Strategies

A good starting point is to break down the statement and identify the assumptions it makes. What is interesting to note in this particular case is the fact that the statement is counter intuitive: it seems to contradict common sense. The nature of the statement makes it suitable for philosophical and psychological arguments

Statement breakdown

a) **We** – general we of humanity

b) **Acquire more knowledge** – knowledge is cumulative – how to quantify it? Is it "true" knowledge? Is it "useful"?

c) **Things –** all encompassing term for the subject of knowledge; vague term: is it only specific things that become less understandable?

d) **Comprehensible** – understandable; how do you gauge a person's understanding? Based on how 'true' it is, or how much it conforms to current scientific trend?

e) **Complex and mysterious** – suggest awe in the face of the vastness of the universe; is it a feeling rather than fact–based speculation?

Assumptions

a) The universe cannot be fully known – the sum of all knowledge cannot be attained

b) Discovering something always opens up new avenues of research

c) Knowledge is measurable – walking in the direction of "true knowledge"

d) We are not 'equipped' to be able to grasp all knowledge

Pros and Cons

Pros

👍 Knowledge is not linear – we also take steps back in our quest for truth

👍 What is 'true' now will end up being proved wrong in the future, as our understanding grows

👍 Knowledge is influenced by society/ dominating paradigms

- 👍 Each new question answered raises other questions
- 👍 More knowledge gained shows us just how complex things are (scientific models always grow in complexity)
- 👍 Our minds are not suitable for understanding the level of complexity of the universe
- 👍 We can only perceive what our senses tell us

Cons

- 👎 Knowledge is quantifiable
- 👎 knowledge is attainable, step by step (knowledge building)
- 👎 Not 'understanding" is a feeling – psychological effect
- 👎 Should not compare current knowledge with sum of all knowledge – but with how little we knew in the past (progress measured by how far we have come, not how far we still have to go)
- 👎 People feel overwhelmed by how much there is still to discover/ the vastness of the universe – it is a psychological effect (fallacy of insignificance)
- 👎 A fully known universe is boring – and that is frightening
- 👎 Average human intelligence has grown significantly
- 👎 High level, complex knowledge is attained by the brilliant and then parsed down
- 👎 We don't only accumulate information but also know how to process and understand it – we don't gather information for information's' sake

Examples:

a) Scientific discoveries can prove how much we know or do not know about the universe

b) Psychology can show how our mind reacts to the universe, its vastness, and how human minds are able to process knowledge and complex issues

c) Philosophy – the study of epistemology (understanding knowledge and how it is acquired)

d) Researchers – what do the foremost minds involved in the knowledge gathering process think about it

e) Biochemistry – abilities or limitations of the human mind

f) Books and movies that have explored the theme before

Lastly, spend a few minutes coming up with a roadmap. While at first it will slow you down, once you become adept at outlining, your writing speed will increase, and your essay will benefit from having a logical structure.

Sample Essay

The universe has always fascinated us – from the very dawn of civilization, when everything seemed shrouded in mystery and the unexplainable was the realms of the gods. The curiosity of the human nature is the driving force of our accelerated evolution and the reason why we have developed methods of systematic study – so that we are better able to understand and control our surroundings. As Sir Francis Bacon said - "knowledge is power".

At the heart of knowledge is the search for truth; of the many ways people try to unravel the mysteries of the universe, scientific research is deemed to be a more accurate understanding of the world. That is because, in essence, scientific research is based on gathering observable and measurable evidence by formulating and testing hypothesis in reproducible experiments. Epistemology, the study of knowledge and how it is acquired, shows us that knowledge gathering is a cumulative process – new theories, no matter how revolutionary, have a basis in previous theories.

Saying that things become more complex and mysterious as we acquire more knowledge means operating under the false assumption that progress is measured by how much we have yet to discover. When humanity is at the start of the line, in terms of understanding the universe and its secrets, progress should be measured by how far we have come, not how far we still have to go. We should not compare our current knowledge with the sum of all knowledge, but rather with how little we knew in the past. Take, for instance, biology and how much we have progressed from believing that human sickness is a result in the imbalance of humors, to the current day advanced understanding of organs, tissues, cells – down to the DNA level. The same can be said for the rudimentary notions of geography of the past, namely the idea that the Earth was flat and that the Sun was orbiting around it. Comparing these notions to the current understanding of tectonics, landscape formation and astrophysics theories like the existence of dark mater, we can see how far our understanding of the universe has progressed, one step at a time. And while we can in no way say that we know everything that there is to know, we can certainly say that we are able to accomplish so much more than in the past, all thanks to a better understanding of our environment.

As such, the amount of knowledge the average individual possesses, has been steadily growing over the ages – the same can be said for our comprehension. What children learn and are able to grasp in schools today would have been part of the mystery of the universe in the past. This increase in knowledge was observed by Buckminster Fuller and named "the Knowledge Doubling Curve". He noticed that until 1900 human knowledge doubled approximately every century and by the end of World War II knowledge was doubling every 25 years. If one were able to travel through time to a period like the Middle Ages, our knowledge, technology, behaviors and speech would be seen as witchcraft. Like Arthur C. Clarke said: 'Magic's just science that we don't understand yet.'

Part of the issue of thinking that the universe becomes progressively incomprehensible is our wonder with the universe, which, while understandable, also inspires the idea that true knowledge is somehow unattainable. People feel overwhelmed by the vastness and complexity of the universe and hold the belief that our simple mind cannot comprehend it - this psychological phenomenon is called the fallacy of insignificance. Colin Wilson in The Stature of Man claims that this fallacy is an effect of modern day society that conditions individuals to lack self-worth, as a mechanism of ensuring compliance – people want to become part of the system, in order to escape their feelings on unimportance. People end up operating on the idea that as an individual, they do not matter much in the grand scheme of things, which is why they should belong to something greater that gives their existence meaning.

Last, but not least, people want to believe that the universe maintains its shroud of mystery because the idea of attaining full, complete knowledge is frightening – a fully known universe is predictable and boring, like professor Farnsworth from Futurama stipulates: : "And, now that I've found all the answers, I realize that what I was living for were the questions!"

Issue Task 6

> *To understand the most important characteristics of a society, one must study its major cities.*
>
> Write a response in which you discuss the extent to which you agree or disagree with the statement and explain your reasoning for the position you take. In developing and supporting your position, you should consider ways in which the statement might or might not hold true and explain how these considerations shape your position.

Strategies

Restate the issue, perhaps by reversing the order of the sentence components.

In other words:

Studying a society's major cities leads to understanding its most important characteristics.

Determine what question is being answered by the statement. This will help you begin to think how you would answer it and whether or not you agree with the original statement.

How can one understand the most important characteristics of a society?

Parts of the original statement that provide evidence that you can affirm or refute.

   a) **understand** – This implies more than identifying or listing. Understanding occurs at a deeper level.

   b) **most important** – The superlative –most- implies a selection process that eliminates less important characteristics. What process and how was it created?

   c) **society** – this can refer to any social entity, large or small.

   d) **major cities** – Major might refer to size of population, state capitals, centers of industry, number of educational institutions. How were cities identified as major?

   e) **study** – This implies a deep examination. What aspects of these cities should one study to gain understanding of society's most important characteristics?

Next, create a statement that expresses the opposing viewpoint, using language similar to that of the original statement.

Opposing viewpoint:

Studying its major cities is not a means to understanding a society's most important characteristics.

Identify the parts of the opposing statement that provide evidence to refute or affirm. In this case, the evidence is the same as that in the original statement except for the word not.

   a) **not** – In this case, it removes studying major cities as a means of understanding society's most important characteristics. Using this statement forces the writer to develop other means of understanding societal characteristics.

Alternatives

Is there any other way to look at this issue? Can you qualify the original statement in some way? Is it possible to partially agree with the statement?

New viewpoint:

To understand the most important characteristics of a society, one must study its major cities as well as small towns and rural communities.

Identify the parts of the new statement that provide evidence to affirm or refute.

a) **one component** – This suggests that studying major cities does not illuminate all of a society's most important characteristics.

The following essay uses this balanced position. In other words, both major cities and smaller towns or rural areas have qualities that make them repositories of a society's important characteristics. List some examples to use as support. Because the issue does not mention what the important characteristics of a society are, you will have the freedom to suggest what they might be.

Examples:

a) **Diversity** – Cities are the likely repositories of this characteristic. Small towns are more homogeneous.

b) **Culture** – Major cities provide greater access to cultural events and displays, e.g., theater, symphony, museums.

c) **Education** – Access to a wide range of educational institutions exists in major cities.

d) **Self–reliance** – Lack of a variety of products and services makes residents of small towns more self–reliant.

Sample Essay

To claim that one can understand a society's most important characteristics by studying only its major cities ignores all of the other social structures that exist within a country. A country as vast as the United States, for example, is made up of fifty states that act as independent entities in many respects. Within each of those states reside groups of citizens united or divided by race, ethnicity, religion, or social class. Some states do not even have what may be considered a major city. To presu.me that only major cities are worthy of study minimizes the contribution of smaller constructs to the characteristics of the larger society. On the other hand, many large cities are composed of smaller societies that may represent those that exist in the remote and far-flung areas of this large country.

Before determining where examples of a country's most important characteristics reside, one would need to identify what those characteristics are. If diversity is near the top of the list, then major cities would be the places to study it. New York City is home to neighborhoods like Little Italy, Chinatown, Spanish Harlem, and Hell's Kitchen. Additionally, residents of NYC live in neighborhoods that cater to lifestyle or economic class, such as Greenwich Village, SoHo, and Park Avenue. Small towns in rural America tend towards homogeneity, and their residents have little exposure to racial or ethnic diversity.

An appreciation for fine arts might rank high in importance as a societal characteristic, and, once again, cities are home to myriad institutions where the fine arts are displayed or performed. Only in major cities is one likely to find museums of art, symphonies, opera houses, and theaters for the live performance of plays and musicals. Residents of small towns may only have a high school band and access works of art on the Internet, thus limiting their exposure to and appreciation of the fine arts.

Physical access to institutions of higher learning elevates the citizens of a society and is universally considered to be important. Graduates of small town high schools must generally leave home to obtain a college degree, whereas students in a major city need travel only a few blocks to attend an Ivy League college, a state university, a design institute, or a school for the performing arts. Lack of access may even discourage children in remote areas from attending college, reducing the overall level of education in those towns and making them less desirable to study for identifying the important characteristics of society.

In contrast, small cities and rural towns may be better locations to study characteristics that are as important as the ones cited above. Residents of these communities are more likely to combine their efforts to support a member in need. One cannot miss the donation cans on convenience store counters that are used for collecting money to help a family that has lost everything to a fire or has a child undergoing expensive medical treatment. The local grocer has a community bulletin board where service clubs can post upcoming events to raise funds to send the high school baseball team to Florida for spring training or to build new dugouts at the town's playground. If concern for one's neighbors ranks high on the list of important characteristics, then small towns are suitable subjects of study.

Residents of rural towns retain some level of self-sufficiency, although the expansion of the Internet has had some impact on that quality. Vegetable gardens are common, and housewives still can and freeze their yields for future consumption. Husbands are jacks-of-all-trades. They mow their own lawns, paint their own houses, and use their own tools to repair broken machines or change a washer on a faucet. Kids on farms have chores as well as school work to complete each day. An important characteristic of any society might be hard work combined with ingenuity, and small towns are likely to be populated with people who display this.

On the whole, the original statement has veracity. Major cities are microcosms; their residents are representative of the society as a whole. Visitors to those cities can see people from all walks of life, from varied backgrounds and those who display talents and abilities that one may find isolated in smaller towns. Cities are growing while small towns are shrinking, so the important characteristics that were once unique to rural America are making their way into cities. However, when attempting to understand an entire society, one must examine all of its communities, including small towns and rural villages. Knowing the criteria used to create the original position would make affirming or refuting it a simpler task.

Issue Task 7

Claim: Governments must ensure that their major cities receive the financial support they need in order to thrive.

Reason: It is primarily in cities that a nation's cultural traditions are preserved and generated.

Write a response in which you discuss the extent to which you agree or disagree with the claim and the reason on which that claim is based.

Strategies

Combine the claim and reason into one statement using a subordinate clause.

In other words:

Because it is in cities that a nation's cultural traditions are preserved and generated, governments must ensure that their major cities receive the financial support they need in order to thrive.

What are the assumptions in the claim and reason? These will provide evidence that you can either affirm or refute in your argument.

a)   Cities generate and preserve most of a nation's cultural traditions.

b)   Small towns and rural areas do not generate or preserve a nation's cultural traditions.

c)   Cities are unable to thrive without financial support from the government.

d)   Cultural traditions should be preserved.

e)   Funding cities in order to preserve cultural traditions is a valuable use of government money.

Next, create a statement that expresses an opposing point of view, using language similar to that in the original statement.

Opposing viewpoint:

Claim: Governments must ensure that communities of all sizes receive the financial support they need to thrive.

Reason: All communities help to generate and preserve a nation's cultural traditions.

What are the assumptions in the claim and reason? These will provide evidence that you can either affirm or refute in your argument.

a)   No type of community should be ignored as a preserver of cultural traditions.

b)   Cities and small towns should receive equal financial support as preservers of cultural traditions.

c)   Some cultural traditions may disappear if certain types of communities are allowed to flounder financially.

Is there any other way to look at this issue? Can you qualify the original statement in some way? Is it possible to partially agree with the statement?

Alternative view:

Claim: Governments should not fund their major cities in order to preserve cultural traditions.

Reason: Cultural groups should be responsible for preserving their own traditions.

What are the assumptions in the alternative claim and reason?

a) Governments should not fund the preservation of cultural traditions.

b) Government should fund projects that benefit the greatest number of people rather than small groups of people.

c) Each cultural group should do what it takes to preserve its own traditions.

Sample Essay

America is a country of immigrants. Over the course of this country's brief history, groups or individuals have made their way to our shores to escape persecution, starvation, or any number of disasters. Language, religious, or other barriers led them to seek those from similar backgrounds, creating communities and neighborhoods where many cultural traditions have been preserved through several generations. These are traditions that they carried with them from their countries of origin. As a nation, America has very few original cultural traditions. The most notable of these is Thanksgiving. We also celebrate our own Independence Day on July fourth and Columbus Day in October. They were neither generated in major cities, nor are they preserved exclusively in major cities. Americans generate and preserve cultural traditions in communities both large and small. Whether these traditions help major cities to thrive is questionable, and whether government funding of their preservation is warranted is subject to debate.

I grew up in a part of Maine that had a significant number of people whose ancestors came from Sweden during the last half of the nineteenth century. In fact, my own ancestors made that journey and settled in Stockholm, obviously named for the capital of their homeland. These Swedes were principally farmers, and they cleared the heavily-forested land and grew crops amenable to a short growing season. They established Lutheran churches, married other Swedish immigrants and prepared meals in the Swedish culinary tradition. Eventually mills designed to manufacture products from the abundant timber were built along the stream that ran through town, and Acadian-French people moved to Stockholm to work in the mills. The schools, once populated by children whose surnames were Anderson, Johnson, and Soderberg now included Plourdes, Rossignols, and Doucettes. The inevitable occurred: French people fell in love with and married Swedish people. Today, there may not be more than a handful of residents who can claim unadulterated Swedish blood. Despite the decline in population and the diluting of the bloodlines, the Swedish community celebrates Midsummer every year. To mark the longest day of the year, residents and visitors alike dress in quaint Swedish costumes, decorate and raise a Maypole, perform Swedish folk dances and eat Swedish food. This is accomplished without the infusion of state or federal funds; volunteers from the community do it all. I'm sure it's all lovely. I wouldn't know because I've never attended the festivities. Even though half of my ancestors are of Swedish descent, I have never lived anywhere but America. I am an American, not a Swedish-American, nor, more correctly, a Swedish-Irish-English-Dutch-American. Because cultural traditions are unique to specific religions, races, or ethnicities, they tend to separate people rather than pull them together. These traditions help individual cultures, rather than entire communities, to thrive.

The vitality of America's major cities relies on factors other than the preservation of cultural traditions. Major cities or any community requires a sound infrastructure to ensure its survival. Without sufficient streets in good repair residents cannot go to work during the day or to places of entertainment in the evening. Without an efficient means of delivering water and eliminating waste, cities would become breeding grounds for disease. A lack of electricity would cripple all forms of industry. Major cities must provide access to health care and education to its residents. Any level of financial support on the part of the government should be allocated to projects that make living in major cities more comfortable. When residents are comfortable, they can pursue activities that help their communities to thrive.

Over recent decades, uniquely American cultural traditions have lost their significance. Thanksgiving has been reduced to a day to prepare for Black Friday, the kickoff to the Christmas shopping season. Stores open earlier than normal and offer desirable merchandise at drastically reduced prices. Entire families spend time on Thanksgiving plotting their shopping strategies. They camp out at stores or get up extra early to be first through the doors when they open, often pushing other bargain hunters out of the way. In 2012, some major chain stores actually opened in the evening on Thanksgiving Day. When America's citizens have so little regard for the country's traditions, the government would be unwise to provide funds to major cities in an attempt to preserve them.

Issue Task 8

> *Some people believe that in order to be effective, political leaders must yield to public opinion and abandon principle for the sake of compromise. Others believe that the most essential quality of an effective leader is the ability to remain consistently committed to particular principles and objectives.*
>
> Write a response in which you discuss which view more closely aligns with your own position and explain your reasoning for the position you take. In developing and supporting your position, you should address both of the views presented.

Strategies

Restate the Issue:

Consider each view separately before deciding which of them you most closely agree with.

Point of view 1: Restate the position using negative terminology.

In other words:

Some people believe that political leaders who do not yield to public opinion and fail to compromise cannot be effective.

Think about the question that is being answered by the statement.

What should political leaders do to be effective?

Now identify elements in the statement that can provide evidence for you to affirm or refute.

   a) **Some people** – This implies that there are two sides to the issue. Not all people agree with position 1.

   b) **effective** – To be effective is to have an effect on something or to effect or create a change.

   c) **yield** – To yield is to give up something. Yielding to an opponent is generally to surrender your own ideas.

   d) **public opinion** – One generally thinks of majority opinion in this case. The entire public never seems to share the same opinion.

   e) **abandon** – This is a strong word. Abandoning an object, person, or idea is likely permanent.

   f) **principle** – A principle is akin to an ideal. Principles develop over a period of years and determine what individuals find acceptable or unacceptable.

   g) **sake** – Sake is a synonym for interest or benefit.

   h) **compromise** – In compromise, all parties give up something. The phrase, a strong compromise, is oxymoronic.

Point of view 2: Restate the position using negative terminology.

In other words:

Others believe that the most essential quality of an effective leader is the refusal to abandon principles and objectives to which they are committed.

This statement answers the same question as the first statement does.

Now, identify the elements in this statement that can provide evidence for you to affirm or refute.

   a) **others** – Like some people in the first point of view, others is not inclusive. It could just as easily be some.

   b) **most essential** – This phrase contains redundancies. Essential is the most; nothing is more needed than the essential part.

   c) **consistently committed** – A foolish consistency is the hobgoblin of little minds. Consistently means that circumstances cannot affect one's commitment to an idea, person, etc.

   d) **objectives** – Objectives must be accomplished on the way to reaching a goal.

The directions do not allow for alternative positions. Even though you may not be in complete agreement with either of the positions, you must decide which one most closely matches the way that you think about the issue. Make certain to acknowledge the opposite viewpoint as you develop your response.

Sample Essay

More than a century ago, Ralph Waldo Emerson said that a foolish consistency is the hobgoblin of little minds. When one becomes enamored of an idea or principle, he or she becomes blind to alternatives. It is as though a hobgoblin or little monster has entered the imagination and blocked off new ideas or the ability to see a different perspective. When opposing parties in a debate refuse to acknowledge any value in their opponents' ideas, nothing is accomplished. We certainly see this in the United States Congress today. Poll numbers are on the decline for the President and most senators and representatives because of their inability to get anything done. Compromise may seem like giving in or giving up, but the alternative is to leave problems unsolved.

The United States may have been governed very differently than it is today if it were not for the Great Compromise. In the early days of America, there was heated debate about the way states would be represented in the national government. One plan called for a unicameral congress where the number of representatives from each state would be based on the state's population. This plan favored states with larger populations. The other plan stated that each state should have the same number of representatives, again in a unicameral legislature. This would leave the people in states with larger populations underserved. The Great Compromise created the bicameral system we have today in America. One body, the Senate, is comprised of two senators from each state, creating a body in which each state, regardless of population, is represented equally. The lower house, the House of Representatives, is comprised of representatives from each state based on population. In this manner, most citizens of the United States are served equally by their elected officials.

The world has become increasingly complex since those early days of America and debate still rages in the halls of government in Washington, DC. A flagging economy, rising unemployment, greater numbers of housing foreclosures, threats to entitlement programs, and bank failures have sparked contrasting ideas about fixes for these problems. Citizens watch while their President or senator or congressmen declare to the media that there will be no bill if their own ideas are not included. Those whose terms in congress next year are already making campaign promises with no sufficient plan to pay for those promises.

Therefore, there must be compromise. After all, promise is part of compromise. Those who are retired or near retirement worry about proposed cuts to Social Security and/or Medicare, and the young workers worry about rising taxes to pay for those entitlements and wonder what will be left for them when they reach retirement age. Current and prospective workers worry about the exportation of jobs to other countries while they are trying to pay for their homes or save money to send their children to college. Students in college worry about the debt they will be saddled with after graduation and if there will be jobs for them once they have their sheepskin in hand. The President and Congress should look to the past and see that compromise was the vehicle that placed them in the positions they now have. They must combine their promises for the good of every citizen.

Issue Task 9

> *The best way to teach is to praise positive actions and ignore negative ones.*
>
> Write a response in which you discuss the extent to which you agree or disagree with the statement and explain your reasoning for the position you take. In developing and supporting your position, you should consider ways in which the statement might or might not hold true and explain how these considerations shape your position.

Strategies

Restate the Issue:

This statement tells what one should do. What shouldn't one do?

In other words:

The best way to teach is not to ignore positive actions or draw attention to negative ones.

Determine what question is being answered by the statement.

What is the best approach to teaching?

The question may help you develop alternative points of view. The original statement is only one of several answers to the question.

Now, think about the parts of the original statement that provide evidence that you can affirm or refute.

a) **best** – This is the superlative form of good. Nothing can surpass it.

b) **praise** – Does the praise have to be verbal? It might be a gold star on a chart or a special privilege.

c) **positive actions** – Positive may be subjective and unclear in the mind of the child. Do the actions have to be physical, or can they include doing well on a test or handing homework in when it is due? It might be volunteering to help another student or cleaning the blackboard.

d) **ignore** – To ignore something is to pretend it doesn't exist.

e) **negative [actions]** – What is negative depends on the teacher's values. Again, are these overt behavioral issues or do they include failing a test or not turning in work?

Opposing viewpoint:

The best way to teach is to expect positive actions and correct negative ones.

Now think about the parts of the opposing statement that provide evidence that you can affirm or refute.

a) **expect** – It is sometimes true that, if you expect children to be well behaved, they will be. The opposite can be true as well; expect bad behavior and you will probably get it.

b) **correct** – Some children have not been taught or modeled good behavior. They need to have their bad actions corrected. This does not necessarily imply punishment.

Alternatives

Is there another way to look at this issue? Can the original statement be qualified in some way?

New viewpoint:

Modeling good behavior is the best way to obtain it from others.

Identify the parts of the alternative statement that can provide evidence for you to refute or affirm.

a) **modeling** –This implies setting an example. If a teacher is polite, her students are likely to imitate that behavior. If she is inconsistent, children will be confused and not know how to behave.

Sample Essay

Every child's first school is his home, and his parents are his first teachers. Whether a child is raised by one or both parents, step parents, grandparents, or foster parents, the child observes and, in most cases, imitates the behaviors of those adults. This imitation is so important that parents often say to their children, "Do as I say, not what I do" when they fear that they may be setting a bad example. A young child's undeveloped brain cannot rely on observation alone to understand how to behave; he or she will make mistakes and act inappropriately from time to time. Occasionally, children need to be corrected.

Children will move on to more formal education around the age of five. Teachers will act in loco parentis, in the place of their parents. Some children enter school with an innate understanding of how to act in this new environment; others will struggle. Teachers have the best interests of their young charges in mind at all times but understand that some children need more direction than others. Ignoring negative actions can actually be dangerous. Running around a classroom, a child can trip and fall or run into a desk, a chair, or another student. Should the teacher be expected to wait until the child tires of running and praise him or her for stopping?

These children will eventually enter the halls of high school where the potential for danger increases tremendously. Chemistry class, alone, has equipment and materials that have the potential to seriously injure those who handle them incorrectly. The teacher who ignores dangerous actions performed by students in this situation should probably be fired. Additionally, there are classes where children may use stoves, irons, pneumatic wrenches, or table saws. For their safety, students must be told when they are using those tools improperly.

Even in classes that are seemingly danger free, accidents can happen. In an otherwise tame English class, students throw pens across the room. These projectiles can end up in another student's eye. Let's not overlook the compasses that students use in math class. Any number of injuries can result from the sharp tip on that instrument.

Teaching continues after children have finished their educations. Employers are not likely to overlook negative actions in the workplace. The bottom line depends on everyone performing his or her job correctly. Children whose negative actions have been ignored throughout their lives will be in for a rude awakening after they leave the safe haven of home and school. Ignoring negative actions may, in the end, be setting children up for future failure.

Issue Task 10

> *Teachers' salaries should be based on their students' academic performance.*
>
> Write a response in which you discuss the extent to which you agree or disagree with the claim. In developing and supporting your position, be sure to address the most compelling reasons and/or examples that could be used to challenge your position.

Strategies

Assumptions:

What are the assumptions in the claim? These are statements that you can either affirm or refute.

Assumption 1: Teachers will become better teachers if their salaries are based on student performance.

Assumption 2: Student performance will improve if teacher salaries are based on that performance.

Assumption 3: Teachers will feel more valued if they are rewarded for being successful.

Assumption 4: Student academic performance – good or bad- depends on teacher pay.

Opposing viewpoint:

Teachers' salaries should not depend on student's academic performance.

What are the assumptions in the opposing claim?

Assumption 1: Teachers' salaries should be determined in the way they have been previously.

Assumption 2: Student performance does not depend on teacher pay.

Assumption 3: Teacher pay should be determined by some criteria other than student performance.

Alternative claim:

Student academic performance should be one of several criteria used to determine a teacher's salary.

Support for alternative claim:

Example: Teachers may lower their standards to allow students to earn better grades. It should not be the only criterion for determining salaries.

Example: Incentives are used in the business world to encourage increased productivity.

Example: Treating student academic performance as a commodity does not take into consideration their individual natures.

Sample Essay

Teacher salaries traditionally depend on a step or seniority system. First-year teachers all make the same salary, as do second-year teachers, and so on. The only way to increase one's salary on any step of the pay scale is to get an advanced degree. Some teachers supplement their salaries by serving as coaches or advisers to school clubs and organizations. All school systems have an evaluation system which does not have an impact on the amount of money an individual teacher makes. Although this system protects teachers from becoming victims of a popularity contest, it also enables incompetent teachers to continue to adversely affect the quality of education delivered to students.

Reform is long overdue, and the criteria for evaluating a teacher's worth must be carefully considered and include more than one critical element. Local school systems, states, and countries are continuously compared with each other based on standardized test scores and other measures of student achievement. Teachers and administrators feel pressured to raise test scores. The unfortunate result can be the cheating scandal that occurred in Georgia earlier this year, when teachers and principals in some districts changed student answers on a standardized test. The temptation to take this action could increase if teacher pay were based on student achievement.

In addition to standardized test scores, student grades are an indication of student achievement. Most school systems still use numerical averages and letter grades to demonstrate student success. These grades place students on honor rolls that are generally published in local newspapers which parents can point to with pride, and they determine class standing, a piece of information requested on college applications. If higher grades are a sign of teacher effectiveness and affect teacher pay, teachers may be tempted to lower their standards to make it easier for their students to earn those higher grades. Student achievement can be used to determine teacher effectiveness and, perhaps, pay, but there first needs to be a better means of measuring and reporting student success.

In the world of business, employees are often rewarded monetarily for their success in meeting or exceeding goals. In most of those cases, workers are producing or selling items that are easily made identical. Quality control is a matter of insuring that each item will perform in the way it was designed to. This is a process impossible to replicate when the product is a human being. Teachers can present the same lessons in the same way year after year and have different results in terms of student success every year. The characteristics of each year's cohort are different. Therefore, achievement will be different.

Teachers do need to be held accountable for student learning. They also need to be evaluated in a manner that fosters and encourages professional growth. When teachers are given a clear direction in which to proceed, they will take their students along. Educational leaders would serve their schools, their states, and their countries well if they ceased comparing their achievements with others. Teacher pay cannot be based on achievement that is loosely defined or compared to test scores in other parts of the state, country, or world.

Issue Task 11

> *College students should base their choice of a field of study on the availability of jobs in that field.*
>
> Write a response in which you discuss the extent to which you agree or disagree with the claim. In developing and supporting your position, be sure to address the most compelling reasons and/or examples that could be used to challenge your position.

Strategies

Assumptions:

What are the assumptions in the claim?

Assumption 1: Some courses of study are more valuable than others.

Assumption 2: Students should not persue what they love if it does not lead to ready employment.

Assumption 3: Some careers are more highly valued than others.

Assumption 4: These careers will always be in high demand.

Opposing viewpoint:

College students should not base their choice of field on the availability of jobs in that field.

What are the assumptions in this claim?

Assumption 1: College students should study what they love.

Assumption 2: College students should base their choice of a field of study on their strengths.

Assumption 3: All jobs are valuable.

Is there another way of looking at the claim? What reason would someone have for making this claim?

Reason 1: Students will need immediate employment to pay off accumulated college debt.

Reason 2: Jobs are more plentiful and readily available in some fields.

Alternative claim

College students must be encouraged to choose a field of study that interests them and addresses their personal and academic strengths.

Support for alternative claim:

Example: Nurses and nurse practitioners are in great demand today. If a student has great difficulty with the sciences, he or she will find it virtually impossible to complete a nursing program successfully. What happens to the job market if colleges and universities produce a surplus of nurses?

Sample Essay

The ranks of the unemployed are filled with people of all ages and all levels of education who believed that, if you work hard, you will be successful. They never could have envisioned the day when their skills would become obsolete or their jobs would be sent to another country where the overhead is lower. They may very well have listened to the advice presented in the original claim when they were going off to college. With visions of dollar signs filling their heads, they enrolled in programs that guaranteed employment post graduation. They were simply being practical. Therefore, students should not pick their undergraduate majors based on the careers available at that moment, because there is no guarantee that those careers will still be available once they graduate.

One can imagine parents today telling their children to follow the words of the claim. In the second decade of the twenty-first century, practicality seems more important than ever. The cost of college discourages students from always following their dreams. Left with college debt that may range from $20,000 to more than $100,000, students must consider how they will repay the loans. The unemployment rate, as well, drives students into careers that promise an immediate and steady paycheck. Dreams and passions are put on hold.

All prospective college students should know that the demand for employees in specific careers ebbs and wanes. For the past few years, officials have been predicting shortage of teachers as many current teachers will reach retirement age shortly. High-school graduates took this as a call to major in education in college, believing that their skills would be in high demand after graduation. Then the recession hit, and states and local school systems had to make budget cuts, accomplished, in part, by eliminating teaching positions. In Texas, alone, the state eliminated 49,000 teaching positions. Not only are those positions unavailable to new college graduates, the teachers who once filled them are now looking for work. Because baby boomers are nearing old age, jobs in the medical field are plentiful. The classifieds are filled daily with ads for nurses, nurse practitioners, and pharmacists. If new college students focus on those careers in great numbers, they will soon create a glut of medical professionals, and many of them will not find work in their fields.

No matter what students choose to study, they should be made aware that they may have to change careers at some point in their lives. They might as well choose a career they are passionate about. The most important skill they might learn in college is how to learn. In today's changing job market, employees must be prepared to update their skill sets. Advancing technology, by itself, has changed the way that traditional jobs are done today. If college students choose a career with the skills and environment that suit them, they will be good at what they do. Eventually, if not immediately, they will be rewarded financially. Do what you love, and the money will follow. It is said that if you choose a job you love, you will never work a day in your life. The true reward of a career choice may reside in the feeling of satisfaction at the end of the day and leaving work with eagerness to return the next day.

Issue Task 12

> *The increasingly rapid pace of life today causes more problems than it solves.*
>
> Write a response in which you discuss the extent to which you agree or disagree with the statement and explain your reasoning for the position you take. In developing and supporting your position, you should consider ways in which the statement might or might not hold true and explain how these considerations shape your position.

Strategies

Restate the Issue:

In this case, the position is stated in the positive. It tells what the rapid pace of life does. Create a statement that expresses the issue in the negative.

In other words:

The increasingly rapid pace of life does not solve more problems than it causes.

You could also determine what question the statement answers.

What are the results of the increasingly rapid pace of life?

Creating a question may help you formulate alternative answers.

Now think about the parts of the original statement that provide evidence that you can refute or affirm.

a) **increasingly** – This implies that the pace of life is more rapid than it used to be, and that the rate is still increasing.

b) **today** – This may lead to the assumption that the pace of life did not increase before now, that it is a current phenomenon.

c) **more**– This is a comparative word and is almost always followed by 'than'. In this case, there are more problems than solutions.

Opposing viewpoint:

The increasingly rapid pace of life does not cause more problems than it solves.

Or: *The increasingly rapid pace of life today solves more problems than it causes.*

Identify the parts of the opposing statement that provide evidence to affirm or refute.

In this case, they would be the same as in the original statement.

Alternatives

Is there any other way to look at this statement? What would life today be like if the pace were slower? Is this a new phenomenon?

New viewpoint:

The increasingly rapid pace of life today is exciting for those who embrace it but overwhelming for those who do not adapt.

Identify parts of the new statement that can create evidence for you to refute or affirm.

a) **exciting** – This can also mean stimulating. The rapid pace of life may stimulate one's creativity or sense of adventure.

b) **embrace** – To embrace something is to accept it willingly. Embrace has a positive connotation.

c) **overwhelm** – Being overwhelmed means that one's abilities or emotions are unable to handle an event.

d) **adapt**– Adaptation is essential to the theory of evolution. Those who fail to adapt do not thrive.

Position:

The increasingly rapid pace of life today creates both obstacles and opportunities.

Examples of obstacles:

a) Some people feel compelled to try to keep up with everything. They stretch themselves too thin.

b) Cultures are losing their unique qualities thanks to rapid travel and communication.

c) The rapid pace tries people's ability to adapt.

Examples of opportunities:

a) Medical research is closing in on cures for deadly and debilitating diseases.

b) The world has become a global village thanks to rapid travel and communication.

Sample Essay

Since the onset of the Industrial Revolution, people have complained about the pace of change and bemoaned the "good old days". In the beginning, man and horsepower were replaced in the fields and on the roads by machines that could perform tasks more quickly and efficiently. Men who were no longer needed in the fields found work in the factories building the machines that had taken their places. Communication kept pace with automation. The telegraph gave way to the telephone, and, when the Atlantic cable was laid, communication with other continents became possible. Man discovered the ability to travel above the earth, and, eventually, people could cross the oceans in a matter of hours rather than weeks. Men and women around the world seized the opportunity to take advantage of these changes and believed that, if they built a better mousetrap, the world would beat a path to their doors.

Some retreated from this progress, seeing all of this technology as a distraction from the true meaning of life. Some, like Thoreau, did it for philosophical reasons, and others, like the Amish, did it for religious reasons. Others could not afford to participate in this revolution and continued to survive using their wits. Pockets of resistance exist to this day, populated by survivalists who see the advances of the late twentieth and early twenty first century as signs of impending doom. These groups are heavily armed and supplied with sufficient provisions to fight off and holdout against those who, they are convinced will someday attack them. Others have taken a gentler approach and simply desire to live by the sweat of their own brows.

The conundrum remains. Does one accept and attempt to keep pace with change, or does one retreat from change and adhere to a simpler philosophy? The downside of the rapid pace is reflected in the busy lives that family members lead, leaving little time to spend "quality" time together. Couples with children frequently maintain a giant calendar in the kitchen on which they keep track of each person's daily activities to schedule who must be where and when. Mothers and fathers separately take their children to before-school practices and after-school or weekend games, recitals or other competitions. Children play at least one sport per season, take dance or karate classes, belong to Boy Scouts or Girl Scouts, and work at a part-time job. Amid these activities, they must complete school work. Rarely are all family members at home at the same time except to sleep. It's a rat race.

On the upside are the advances that benefit humans. The rapid pace of medical research has led to successful treatments for a variety of deadly and/or debilitating diseases. It was not so long ago that a cancer diagnosis was a death sentence. Today, many cancers are curable, and lives have been extended. Smallpox has been erradicated, and vaccines exist that promise the same end for diseases that used to scar or kill those who contracted them. A future free of cervical cancer can only be promising for the women of the world. Advances in communication have made knowledge of new discoveries readily available around the world. Ultimately, individuals must discriminate between activities and advances that enhance their lives. The problems created by the increasingly rapid pace of life today are likely created by the choices that individuals make for themselves.

Issue Task 13

> *Universities should require every student to take a variety of courses outside the student's field of study.*
>
> Write a response in which you discuss the extent to which you agree or disagree with the recommendation and explain your reasoning for the position you take. In developing and supporting your position, describe specific circumstances in which adopting the recommendation would or would not be advantageous and explain how these examples shape your position.

Strategies

Restate the Position:

You may create a version that negates the original in more than one way.

In other words:

Universities should not allow students to take only courses in their fields of study.

You could also determine the question that is being answered by the recommendation.

What kinds of courses should colleges require their students to take?

Or: *How can universities ensure that they are turning out well educated graduates?*

Creating a question can help you think about the way that you would answer it. Consider what you would deem to be the composition of a good college education.

Now think about the parts of the original recommendation that provide evidence that you can affirm or refute.

 a)   **require** – This allows for no alternative. One must fulfill a requirement. How many and what types of courses should universities require? Should they require any courses?

 b)   **every** – Again, there is no option.

 c)   **variety** – Variety implies more than one type. How many types of courses should universities require outside a student's field of study?

 d)   **outside** – How far outside? If one is studying literature, should he or she be required to take chemistry?

Opposing viewpoint:

Universities should not require every student to take a variety of courses outside the student's field of study.

Identify the parts of the opposing statement that provide evidence to affirm or refute. In this case, the only new word is *not*, and it simply serves to negate the original statement.

Alternatives

Is there any other way to look at this statement? Should colleges require students to take a variety of courses before they declare a major? Should requirements exist only within a course of study?

New viewpoint:

College and universities should require enough courses to complete a field of study to ensure that a student is sufficiently educated in that field.

Identify the parts of the opposing statement that provide evidence to affirm or refute.

a) **enough** – What is enough? Are there options for gaining a degree in a field of study?

b) **ensure** – This means to make certain. Is it a college's responsibility to make sure that a student takes the courses he or she will need to satisfy a degree in a field of study?

c) **sufficiently** – This is similar to enough. What does it mean to be sufficiently educated? Should it be enough to gain employment in the field?

Position:

Universities should require every student to take a variety of courses outside the student's field of study.

Examples and reasons:

a) At the beginning of a student's college career, he may not know the field in which to major. The student may discover an area of interest in the variety of courses required during the first two years of college.

b) A student may discover an avocation while taking a variety of courses. A required course in art history may lead to a life long passion for collecting fine art or visiting museums around the world.

c) The workplace is always changing. One may find himself out of work at some point, and a required course outside of his field may lead him to a new career.

Sample Essay

Universities offer courses in a wide variety of disciplines. At some point, generally by the end of the second year, students are required to declare a major. In some cases, students begin classes in a program of study from the minute they enter the university. Some college freshmen seem to have been called to a profession at an early age, and their determination to become a teacher, or doctor, or engineer has never wavered. On the other hand, most freshmen are waiting for the fires of inspiration to be lit. The surest way to accomplish that is to take a variety of courses in a range of disciplines. It is a fact that, in the United States, only 1 in 4 college students graduates in four years. The greatest number finishes after five years of college, usually because they changed their majors along the way. It is unrealistic to expect today's seventeen or eighteen-year-olds, whose life expectancies are around eighty-five years, to decide what they want to do for the rest of their lives. Gone are the days that an individual will obtain a job in a company and remain there for his or her entire working life. Surveys reveal that the average working person today changes careers every ten years. What career selection he or she makes may derive from a course taken in college. Limiting what courses a student takes in college may limit his or her career choices later in life.

On the other hand, the job market today is a mine field. If some college student missteps, his or her chances for a career may blow up. Some students may be frustrated by a requirement to take courses outside their fields of study. Their focus on taking as many courses as possible in the field they wish to pursue may be impressive in the job application process. College students may feel that their exposure to a variety of courses in high school is sufficient, so repeating that in college is redundant.

At a traditional university, a student will enroll in five courses per semester; that's a total of forty classes in four years. Narrowing one's choices could have disadvantages. It is realistic to assume that a student could burn out from the lack of variety. The courses may be taught by professors who fail to expire, and those professors may teach all of the courses in the field. After a couple of years, the student may decide that he or she made a mistake in choosing it and now has no option but to continue to the bitter end or start from scratch.

Universities should require students to take a variety of courses in several disciplines. Courses that teach the nuts and bolts in any field generally are offered to college juniors and seniors, anyway. At the end of the college career, a student will have the skills and knowledge he or she needs to pursue a career beyond college, as well as exposure to areas of knowledge that might spark a lifelong interest in some hobby or other avocation.

Issue Task 14

> *If a goal is worthy, then any means taken to attain it are justifiable.*
>
> Write a response in which you discuss the extent to which you agree or disagree with the statement and explain your reasoning for the position you take. In developing and supporting your position, you should consider ways in which the statement might or might not hold true and explain how these considerations shape your position.

Strategies

Restate the Issue:

Restate the issue by making the phrasing of it in the negative.

In other words:

No means of attaining a goal should be overlooked if the goal is worthy.

You could also determine what question is being answered by the issue statement.

Should any and all means possible be used to obtain a worthy goal?

Or: *Is any goal worth achieving at any cost?*

These questions may help you think about how you would answer them. Your answers can help you develop your response to the issue.

Now think about the parts of the statement that provide evidence that you can refute or affirm.

a) **worthy** – Worth of anything, including a goal, is subjective. If everyone believed all goals are worthy, there would be no need to take any extraordinary or unjustifiable action to reach the goal.

b) **any means** – This is expansive. In this case, any can mean all.

c) **justifiable** – To justify something is to explain or excuse it. Should we do anything that needs an explanation or excuse?

Opposing viewpoint:

No goal is worth enough to justify taking any means to attain it.

Identify the parts of the opposing statement that provide evidence to affirm or refute.

a) **no** – In this case, it means none. This is pretty definitive.

Alternatives

Is there any other way to look at this issue? In this case, it may be difficult. The original statement already qualifies the statement by using the word, if. The original statement is essentially saying that some goals are worth any means of achieving, and the opposing viewpoint says that no goals are worth that risk.

Position:

No goal is worth enough to justify taking any means to attain it.

Examples and reasons:

a) **Guantanamo** – Suspected terrorists are imprisoned at Guantanamo Bay, a military institution owned by the United States in Cuba. These prisoners have been subjected to water boarding, a particularly inhumane form of torture. Is information about terrorist activities important enough to justify torture?

Sample Essay

To justify an action is to make it seem just or fair. It implies that the action is done to right a wrong. It is akin to the biblical philosophy, an eye for an eye. On the other hand, two wrongs don't make a right. Are any goals so lofty that one can justify taking any action to reach them? Is it okay to take these actions in the name of God or in the spirit of patriotism? Events of the past decade may make one believe that reprisals are justifiable.

Atrocities of such magnitude have been committed by groups or individuals around the world throughout history, that one might agree that any means used to eliminate these perpetrators is justified. In 2001, extremists Muslims used the piloting skills they had learned in a flight school in the United States to fly two passenger planes into the towers of the World Trade Center in New York City, one into the Pentagon, and another aimed at the White House that went crashing into a field in Pennsylvania. These events caused the war on terrorism to be a focal point of US foreign policy. It became the goal of the United States military to hunt down and kill or capture the leaders of terrorist cells around the world. Chief among those targets was Osama bin Laden. In May 2011, an elite group of Seals burst into his home and killed him. The US government presented this as an incredible accomplishment – which it was – that was worth the efforts needed to reach it. However, this is not necessarily true.

To reach this end, the United States invaded Iraq, believing that Saddam Hussein's regime had caches of WMDs, Weapons of Mass Destruction. That turned out to be false, but, nonetheless, the military hunted down and captured Hussein, after which he was tried and executed. During this span of time, other suspected terrorists were rounded up and detained at Guantanamo Bay, a US military institution in Cuba. There, these terrorists were systematically tortured to make them reveal information about the whereabouts of terrorist cells and, likely, bin Laden himself. Among the techniques used to extract information was water boarding, a particularly inhumane process that causes its victims to feel like they are drowning. And then, there's Abu Ghraib, a prison in Iraq, where US military personnel tortured and degraded the inmates held there. Considering the acts perpetrated by these terrorists on American soil, the actions taken by the United States appear justifiable. The flame of patriotism burned brightly and was reflected in the eyes of ordinary citizens and those called to battle. Across the country, acts of terrorism were perpetrated by those ordinary citizens against other citizens of Middle Eastern origin. Young men whose ancestors came here from countries like Syria and Lebanon generations ago were detained and strip searched at border crossings between the US and Canada. People in airports across the country looked askance at fellow passengers who looked or dressed differently. Members of the military who have served in Iraq and Afghanistan are experiencing post-traumatic stress disorder in numbers greater than seen before in our military history.

If the goal is to eradicate terrorism, isn't any action in the cause justifiable? Whenever humans are reduced to treating other human beings inhumanely, we must pause and consider the consequences of attaining this supposedly lofty goal. We must question whether any goal is worth the ultimate price one pays, especially when the actions taken are degrading or debasing to other groups of people, and the price is a loss of human dignity for the perpetrators and the victims.

Issue Task 15

> *In order to become well-rounded individuals, all college students should be required to take courses in which they read poetry, novels, mythology, and other types of imaginative literature.*
>
> Write a response in which you discuss the extent to which you agree or disagree with the recommendation and explain your reasoning for the position you take. In developing and supporting your position, describe specific circumstances in which adopting the recommendation would or would not be advantageous and explain how these examples shape your position.

Strategies

Restate the Issue:

The original statement tells what students should do. Rephrase it by telling what students should not do without changing the meaning of the original statement.

In other words:

In order to become well-rounded individuals, all college students should not finish college without first taking courses in which they read poetry, novels, mythology, and other types of imaginative literature.

Or: *College students will fail to become well-rounded individuals if they are not required to take courses in which they read poetry, novels, mythology, and other types of imaginative literature.*

You could determine what question is being answered by the original issue statement.

What required courses should all college students take in order to become well-rounded individuals?

Thinking about your answer to the question can help you as you develop your response to the original statement.

Now think about the parts of the statement that provide evidence that you can affirm or refute.

a) **well-rounded** – This is both subjective and vague. What does it mean to be well-rounded, and who decides if one is well-rounded? Should the goal of college be to create well-rounded individuals?

b) **all students** – This leaves no room for doubt and no exceptions. The statement assumes that these courses have the power to make all students well-rounded.

c) **required** – A requirement is a need. This is like saying that all college students need these courses to become well-rounded.

d) **other types of imaginative literature** – Isn't most literature imaginative?

Opposing viewpoint:

In order to become well-rounded individuals, all college students should be required to take a variety of courses in several disciplines.

Identify the parts of the opposing statement that provide evidence that you can refute or affirm.

    a) **variety of courses** – Well-rounded individuals may be those that have exposed themselves to a variety of courses in several disciplines.

Alternatives:

Is there any other way of looking at this issue? Can you qualify the original statement in some way? Why wouldn't taking a variety of courses in the social sciences make one a well-rounded individual?

New viewpoint:

In order to become well-rounded individuals, college students shouldn't restrict their selection of academic classes to those within one discipline.

Identify the parts of the new statement that provide evidence to affirm or refute.

    a) **restrict** – This means to limit oneself. A restriction is something one cannot do.

    b) **selection** – Choice and selection are synonymous.

    c) **within one discipline** – This is a narrow perspective. Narrow is contradictory to well-rounded.

Position:

It should not be the goal of colleges and universities to turn out well-rounded individuals.

Support:

    a) **cost** – Education is too costly today for students to focus on courses that have no practical value.

    b) **interest** – By the time a student is in college, he or she should be allowed to choose courses that they have an interest in.

Sample Essay

It is impossible to identify well-rounded individuals on the street, in the workplace, or at the gym. It is unlikely that anyone is choosing his or her friends based on their being well-rounded. It is probably impossible to define well-rounded; everyone would have a point of view. It is true that in the early days of higher education, one aimed to become a "man of letters", knowledgeable to some degree in a variety of subjects. That luxury is no longer desirable or practical. University students are entering a different world.

I like to think of myself as well-rounded. I am interested in a variety of topics, and I participate in a variety of activities. I carry on conversations easily with my friends and family as well as people I meet in the grocery store or at an airport. My seatmates on trains and planes find me engaging. I answer most of the questions on Jeopardy! correctly, and I can complete the New York Times crossword puzzle. I like and can cook food from a variety of cuisines. I can order correctly from a menu written in French. I like HGTV, the Food Network, and action movies. My friends think I'm funny, and I cry over sappy commercials on TV. None of my self-perceived well-roundedness is a result of courses that I either did or did not take in college.

These interests can also stem from outside influences. My mother taught me to knit and sew. I got my love of gardening from my father. I taught myself to read. My sister taught me how to see different perspectives of an issue. I learned to swim during lessons on cold mornings at the local pool. I learned to play the piano from an older lady who tapped out the measures with a plastic knitting needle on the top of the piano. I learned to drive from a kind and patient man who did not use deodorant and wouldn't let his students roll down the car windows in the heat of the summer. My friends taught me about friendship. I obtained all of these skills before I went to college.

So, what did college teach me? College taught me how to live in close quarters with hundreds of other girls from different states and backgrounds. College taught me to understand football, to party on the weekends, and how to join the best sorority on campus. College taught me to sign up for classes that ended by 1:00 pm and met on Mondays, Wednesdays, and Fridays, so I'd have two full days off from classes. College eventually taught me how to manage my time. It taught me the classes I would need to get a degree in my major.

High school seniors plan to enter colleges and universities with the goal of getting a job after graduation, and that is what college should do. When today's high-school seniors graduate from college, they will have enormous debt. While in college, they must focus on courses that serve practical purposes. They will need immediate employment in order to meet their financial obligations. They will become well-rounded by living their lives after college, not by taking a variety of courses in the humanities.

Issue Task 16

> *Politicians should pursue common ground and reasonable consensus rather than elusive ideals.*
>
> Write a response in which you discuss the extent to which you agree or disagree with the recommendation and explain your reasoning for the position you take. In developing and supporting your position, describe specific circumstances in which adopting the recommendation would or would not be advantageous and explain how these examples shape your position.

Strategies

Restate the Issue:

The original statement tells what politicians should do. Create a statement that tells what politicians should not do without changing the meaning of the statement.

In other words:

Politicians should not pursue elusive ideals instead of pursuing common ground and reasonable consensus.

You could also determine what question is being answered by the recommendation.

What is the best way for politicians to serve the electorate?

Now think about the parts of the recommendation that provide evidence that you can affirm or refute.

   a) **common ground** – This implies agreement or standing together.

   b) **reasonable** – This is something that is arrived at by using reason or logic.

   c) **consensus** – The implication is agreement, coming together.

   d) **elusive** – Something elusive is not easily caught or understood. It is slippery.

   e) **ideals** – An ideal is the perfect form of something.

   f) **pursue** – To pursue is to chase or follow.

Opposing viewpoint:

Politicians should avoid common ground and reasonable consensus in the pursuit of elusive ideals.

Identify the parts of the opposing statement that provide evidence that you can refute or affirm.

   a) **avoid** – When avoiding something, you stay away from it.

Alternatives:

Is there any other way to look at the recommendation? Can parts of it be qualified in any way? Should politicians retain some of their ideals while pursuing common ground and reasonable consensus?

New viewpoint:

Politicians should not abandon their ideals as they pursue common ground and reasonable consensus.

Sample Essay

Men and women enter the political arena ready to do battle against special interest groups and pork barrel spending. They've promised their constituents that they're going to clean up that mess in Washington or the capital in the state they serve. The voters are confident they've elected someone who will stick to his or her guns. Without dreams of making a change for the better, politicians would not exist. But as poet Robert Burns said, 'The best laid plans of mice and men often go awry." It doesn't take long for politicians to realize that their individual voices aren't very loud, or that they may not have a full understanding of the policy that they are attempting to argue.

Everyone who chooses politics as a career must possess at least a modicum of naiveté. If the candidate didn't think he or she could make a difference, there would be no reason to run for office. Changing the world is a lofty goal, but it is generally accomplished at a snail's pace and one compromise at a time. We learn to compromise as young children. Our parents tell us if we clean our rooms, we can have a treat. If compromise means that both sides give up something to get something, then the deal we made with Mom is compromise. We give up some free time to clean our rooms and get in return more TV time or a candy bar. Mom gives up some peace and quiet but gets a clean room.

Political compromise is more difficult to achieve, and the stakes are higher. The principle, however, is the same. Reaching a consensus takes a little sleight of hand and a gift for rhetoric. The idealistic politician may have to temper his or her enthusiasm when choosing from the list of persuasive techniques at hand to lead his fellow politicians to common ground. This politician must keep the constituents in mind as he seeks the consensus that will allow him to retain his ideals. Today, in the halls of Congress and in the White House, there is great debate about the budget. Senators and congressmen on both sides of the debate are finding it difficult to find common ground. The ideals of some make them refuse to consider raising taxes for any citizens in America, while others believe that the wealthy should pay more taxes. Some feel so protective towards the poor and the elderly that they refuse to make cuts in any of the tax-funded programs that serve those groups, while others say that those programs must be reduced in scope to protect everyone. It is sometimes difficult for citizens watching this debate to determine if their representatives in Washington are holding steadfast to the ideals they took with them to Congress, or if they are spouting the rhetoric they believe will get them reelected.

All politicians, whether on the local, state, or national level would do well to revisit the Preamble to the Constitution, whose first line includes the words, "in order to form a more perfect union". Perfect means ideal and union means agreement. Whatever the issue may be, politicians should strive for perfect agreement. In the end, the agreement may not seem perfect to every politician, but it should serve the needs of the people they represent.

Issue Task 17

People should undertake risky action only after they have carefully considered its consequences.

Write a response in which you discuss the extent to which you agree or disagree with the recommendation and explain your reasoning for the position you take. In developing and supporting your position, describe specific circumstances in which adopting the recommendation would or would not be advantageous and explain how these examples shape your position.

Strategies

Restate the Position:

The original recommendation suggests how people should behave regarding risks. How would the recommendation read if it were couched in negative terms?

In other words:

People should not take risks until they have considered the consequences.

The meaning of both recommendations is essentially the same.

You could also determine what question is being answered by the recommendation.

Should individuals take risks?

Or: *Under what conditions should people take risks?*

Now think about the parts of the recommendation that provide evidence that you can affirm or refute.

   a) **only** – This leaves no other option. It is akin to saying always. Are there no exceptions?

   b) **risky** – This can be relative. What may appear risky to one may be commonplace for another.

   c) **carefully** – The meaning of carefully can vary, as well. How much consideration is considered careful?

   d) **considered** – To consider something is to think about it. it does not require taking any action. Does one only need to think about the consequences of one's actions? Does understanding the consequences prevent everyone from engaging in risky behavior? Does consideration necessarily lead to understanding?

Opposing viewpoint:

People should undertake risky action regardless of the consequences.

Think about the parts of the opposing statement that provide evidence to affirm or refute.

   a) **regardless** – This means without regard. To regard something is to look at it. One should take risks without looking at the consequences.

b)   **should** – This is not a command. *Should* imply choice.

Alternatives:

Is there another way to look at this recommendation? Can it be qualified? Are some risks worth taking despite the possible consequences? Can risks be minimized?

New viewpoint:

Even with the possibility of negative consequences, some risks are worth taking.

Examples and reasons:

a)   **Marie and Pierre Curie** – When they began experimenting with radiation, the risks were unknown. Marie Curie died from radiation sickness, but her contribution to the advancement of medicine is immeasurable.

b)   **early explorers**– When the Vikings set out in their boats and headed west, they could not imagine what they would find. They found rich fishing grounds. Columbus, Cook, Drake, Magellan all risked their lives to set out across seas that no man had navigated before.

c)   **space exploration**

d)   **Bill Gates and Steve Jobs** – Both are pioneers in computing technology, Gates with software and Jobs with McIntosh computers

Sample Essay

Some people are born risk takers. Psychologists will tell you that it is component of one's personality, and those who take risks sometimes exhibit negative behavior while others take risks that ultimately benefit themselves and others. The names of risk takers can be found in various halls of fame as well as on Wanted Posters. Famous risk takers range from the infamous like Al Capone and Bernie Maid off to the innovators like Bill Gates, Mark Zuckerberg, and Frank Lloyd Wright. Even though these and others knew the possible consequences of their actions, they were not deterred from reaching their goals. Those who do not take risks will not suffer the possible negative consequences, but neither will they experience the rewards.

Where would we be without those who took great risks with general disregard for the consequences? Marie and Pierre Curie literally risked their lives to experiment with radioactivity. The medical progress that resulted from their work not only earned the Curies the Noble Prize but made possible early treatment of some cancers. Other scientists followed in their footsteps, and the benefits to mankind have been enormous. Other medical pioneers include Jonas Salk who saved countless children from death or paralysis when he tested his new polio vaccine on himself, his wife and his own children. Risking his and his family's lives led to mass administration of the vaccine to school children all over America, and virtually made the iron lung obsolete.

Early explorers risked traveling to areas marked on maps with the foreboding phrase, "Here there are dragons", and expanded the known world. In efforts to find a shorter route to India, sailors like Christopher Columbus set off with his crew in three small boats and bumped into the Western Hemisphere. Charles Lindbergh flew solo across the Atlantic in a small plane in hopes of reaching the European continent. Since that time, man has used flight to reach the moon and establish space stations. If these adventurers had spent too much time thinking about the consequences, they may very well have just stayed home.

In the later years of the twentieth century pioneers in technology arose. Bill Gates, founder of Microsoft and one of the richest men in the world, dropped out of prestigious Harvard University to pursue computing. Steve Jobs, the brains behind Apple computers, also dropped out of college. These men defied the popular wisdom that one needs a college education to get anywhere in this world and created a universe of communication on a level never before seen.

Great political leaders have taken great risks for the sake of reform or revolution. Martin Luther King, Jr and Mohandas Gandhi (after whom King modeled his protests), risked everything and, ultimately, lost their lives for the sake of equality and independence. Both men certainly considered the consequences of their actions but deemed that the potential rewards made the risks acceptable. All minorities and repressed populations in the United States lead lives of greater opportunity thanks to the leadership of Martin Luther King, Jr, and India exists as an independent country as a result of Gandhi's actions.

Just as there are consequences for taking risks, there are consequences for failing to take risks. Those who fear the unknown are doomed to live meager lives. It may be trite but nonetheless true to say that if you do what you've always done, you'll get what you've always had.

Issue Task 18

Leaders are created by the demands that are placed on them.

Write a response in which you discuss the extent to which you agree or disagree with the statement and explain your reasoning for the position you take. In developing and supporting your position, you should consider ways in which the statement might or might not hold true and explain how these considerations shape your position.

Strategies

Restate the Issue:

This statement tells how leader are created. How they are not created?

In other words:

Leaders do not arise until demands have been placed on them.

Determine what question is being answered by the issue statement.

How are leaders created?

Or: *Under what conditions do leaders emerge?*

How would you answer the questions? Your answer will help you develop your response to the statement.

Now think about the parts of the statement that provide evidence that you can affirm or refute.

   a) **created** – This assumes that leaders are made and not born. There must be some process by which leaders come to be.

   b) **demands** – These are like orders. One cannot avoid or ignore a demand.

   c) **placed upon them** – This implies a lack of choice.

Opposing viewpoint:

Leaders arise through some preparation to lead.

Identify the parts of the opposing statement that provide evidence that you can refute or affirm.

   a) **Arise** – This implies that those that are prone to leadership will assume it when the situation requires.

   b) **preparation** – Leaders don't appear spontaneously. Through some desire or proclivity for leadership, they have prepared to assume it when called upon.

Is there another way to look at this issue? Are some leaders reluctant to lead? Are they leading by default? Did they assume a leadership role out of a sense of responsibility rather than the desire to lead? Do some seek leadership? Can the two stated viewpoints be combined?

New viewpoint:

Some leaders are forced into that position by circumstances, while others develop leadership skills over a lifetime.

Identify the parts of the new viewpoint that provide evidence for you to refute or affirm.

a) **Some** – This leaves room for exceptions. It is not all.

b) **forced** – This suggests a lack of willingness to lead. There may be no options.

c) **circumstances** – This is the same as a situation. The implication is the situation is unexpected.

d) **develop** – Development implies growth. Some leaders have grown into more sophisticated leadership abilities.

e) **lifetime** – Real leadership isn't something that happens overnight. As situations change, leaders learn to adapt.

Position:

Some leaders are forced into that position by circumstances, while others develop leadership skills over a lifetime.

Examples and Reasons:

a) **The lost battalion** – Major Whittlesey's sudden elevation to military leadership

b) **Flight 93** – Regular citizens taking over in a crisis.

c) **Military generals** – They are career leaders.

Sample Essay

Leadership positions are best filled by people whose nature enables them to endure both the successes and failures that accompany the challenges a leader will face. Some leaders are made by their circumstances, which push them to acquire traits that they may not have otherwise. This leadership can be transient – that is, leaders can be made by a particular situation and then return to their non-leadership position once the situation has been handled. History contains many examples of all such leaders.

When the United States entered WWI, Charles Whittlesey, a mild-mannered, Harvard-educated lawyer was commissioned an officer in the US Army. He led a battalion of young infantrymen out of the trenches and into the Argonne Forest in France in an attempt to retake land that was occupied by the Germans. Having been given incorrect information, Major Whittlesey and his men became trapped behind enemy lines where they endured artillery attacks by the Germans who outnumbered them. They even came under friendly fire when the Allies used incorrect coordinates in an effort to attack the Germans with cannon fire. After 5 days, the battalion was rescued. Of the more than 500 men who entered the forest with Whittlesey, fewer than 200 walked out of the forest with him. The remainder had been killed, captured by the enemy, or wounded. After the war ended, Whittlesey, who received the Congressional Medal of Honor for his heroic deeds, returned to the practice of law. Three years later, Charles Whittlesey booked a cruise, and while on that cruise, jumped overboard. Major Whittlesey became a leader through the demands placed upon him. Even though he acted with honor and effectively saved the lives of hundreds of the men in his charge, the loss of so many more weighed so heavily on him that he took his own life.

Renowned leaders have arisen from the ranks of the US armed forces. American history texts recount the exploits of brave men like General Douglas McArthur who promised the people of the Philippines that he would return. General Dwight Eisenhower was the supreme Allied Commander during the invasion of Normandy on D-Day in 1944 and went on to serve two terms as President of the United States. The difference between these men and Charles Whittlesey was their choice of a military career. They embraced the challenges, celebrated the victories, and accepted the loss of life.

On rare occasions, situations do arise that force ordinary citizens to assume leadership and perform extraordinary acts of bravery. Ten years ago, passengers on United Airlines flight 93, after learning what had happened at the World Trade Center in New York City, decided to take action that would prevent their own hijacked plane from causing a similar disaster and stormed the cockpit where terrorists had assumed control of the plane. As a result, the plane that was on a course that would have taken it to the nation's capital, crashed in a field in Pennsylvania, averting disaster while killing everyone on board.

While events occasionally conspire to force individuals into leadership roles, effective, long-term leadership is best left to those whose proclivities cause them to desire the responsibilities of leadership. Reluctant or ineffectual leaders may cause more harm than good, either to themselves or those they are leading.

Issue Task 19

> *The most effective way to understand contemporary culture is to analyze the trends of its youth.*
>
> Write a response in which you discuss the extent to which you agree or disagree with the statement and explain your reasoning for the position you take. In developing and supporting your position, you should consider ways in which the statement might or might not hold true and explain how these considerations shape your position.

Strategies

Restate the Issue:

How can you change the statement without changing its meaning?

In other words:

The least effective way to understand contemporary culture is to ignore the trends of its youth.

Or: *The surest way to misunderstand contemporary culture is to ignore the trends of its youth.*

Determine what question is being answered by the issue statement.

How can one understand contemporary culture?

Creating a question will help you to think about how you would respond. Your answer to the question can help you develop your response to the statement.

Now think about the parts of the statement that provide evidence that you can affirm or refute.

   a) **most effective** – Most is the superlative form of many; nothing is more effective.

   b) **understand** – This statement assumes that one can understand contemporary culture.

   c) **analyze** – Analysis is the process of breaking something down into its components. What are the components of the trends?

   d) **youth** – What age group specifically? Does the term, youth, extend to those in college?

Opposing statement:

The most effective way to understand contemporary culture is not to analyze the trends of its youth.

Identify the parts of the opposing statement that provide evidence that you can refute or affirm.

   a) **not** – In this case, the implication is that one should ignore the trends of a culture's youth. Including those trends might give a false impression of the culture.

Alternatives

Is there another way to look at this issue? Can you qualify the original issue statement in some way?

New viewpoint:

Analyzing the trends of its youth is one component in understanding the contemporary culture.

Identify the parts of the new statement that provide evidence to affirm or refute.

   a)   **one** – This implies that there are others.

   b)   **contemporary** – The culture of this time.

Sample Essay

The culture of any era is defined by a variety of elements and may be the result of past influences. Analyzing the trends of today's youth is only one of those elements. One also needs to analyze the kinds of work that adults are pursuing or the activities its senior citizens are participating in. To rely solely on analysis of youth trends is short-sighted. The youth of a culture are heavily influenced by the latest, hottest fad. Their greatest need is to fit in, to be cool, and they change their clothes, their hair, and their phones as soon as the newest fashion is featured in print or on television. Their permanence is ephemeral, and their influence may be longer lasting. A big chunk of their time would be spent just keeping up. Anyone attempting to analyze the trends of youth will barely finish before the trends change.

The most widely-exposed youth culture of the last half century is that of the 1960's and 70's. The youth of that era advised others to tune in, turn on, and drop out. Drugs, sex and rock and roll permeated the culture of youth in those decades. Because burning draft cards and bras was so widely publicized, it would be tempting to believe that all youth behaved in that manner. That would be a mistake. Despite the presence of SDS chapters, peace rallies and sit-ins on college campuses across the country, most students quietly went about attending classes, graduating and getting traditional jobs. The counterculture of the 60's and 70's had its greatest influence on later decades. Those days of rebellion and revolution led to increased opportunities for minorities and women. The young people of that era are now nearing retirement and are living lives very different from the senior citizens of previous generations. They have tuned in, but they have not dropped out. They are healthier, better educated, and leading more active lives than their parents or grandparents did.

Analysis of youthful trends reveals what effect advertising had on a culture's young people. To fully understand contemporary culture, one must analyze the hopes, fears, and actions of all the groups that comprise it. A culture's youth is blissfully ignorant of a culture's realities. The struggle of adults to find satisfying work, to pay the bills, to provide security for themselves and their children define the attitudes and behaviors of contemporary culture.

Issue Task 20

All parents should be required to volunteer time to their children's schools.

Write a response in which you discuss the extent to which you agree or disagree with the recommendation and explain your reasoning for the position you take. In developing and supporting your position, describe specific circumstances in which adopting the recommendation would or would not be advantageous and explain how these examples shape your position.

Strategies

Restate the Recommendation:

Attempt to use negative words to convey the same meaning as the original.

In other words:

No parent should be exempt from volunteering time to their children's schools.

Determine what question is being answered by the issue statement.

Which parents should be required to volunteer time to their children's schools?

OR: Should all parents be required to volunteer time to their children's schools?

OR: How can parents become more involved in their children's educations?

There may be several other questions that call for the answer in the original recommendation. Answering these questions can help you formulate a response or alternative recommendation. It can help you identify the circumstances in which adopting the recommendation would be advantageous or disadvantageous.

Now think about the parts of the original recommendation that provide evidence that you can affirm or refute.

a) **All parents** – There are no exceptions. What about working parents? Noncustodial parents?

b) **required** – Again, there are no exceptions. It's not an option.

c) **time** – Does it have to be during the school day? This could be interpreted to mean cleaning the classroom on the weekend. Does it have to be time? Could they volunteer to supply snacks or tissues?

d) **volunteer** – To volunteer is to give freely. Require and volunteer contradict each other.

Opposing viewpoint:

Not all parents should be required to volunteer time in their children's schools.

Identify the parts of the opposing statement that provide evidence that you can refute or affirm.

a) **not all** – This implies that some should be required. For which parents should this be a requirement?

Alternatives:

Is there any other way to look at this recommendation? Can it be qualified in some way? Think about the absolute words like all and required. Can they be reduced to less than commands?

New viewpoint:

All parents should be encouraged to volunteer time in their children's schools.

Identify the parts of the new statement that provide evidence to affirm or refute.

a) **all** – This leaves no one out. If volunteerism is encouraged, everyone should be invited to participate.

b) **encouraged** – To encourage would involve building some flexibility into the time frame and types of volunteering required.

Examples and Reasons:

a) **financial** – Budget cuts have adversely affected the ability of teachers and schools to accomplish many tasks that aides or janitors used to do.

b) **transparency** – Volunteering is a great way to know what is happening in a child's school or classroom.

c) **exceptions** – Encouraging rather than requiring leaves an option for parents who have neither the time nor the desire to volunteer in their children's schools.

d) **danger** – Some children have parents who should not volunteer at their children's schools under any circumstances. Some parents are abusive or alcoholics or drug users. Their children are likely to feel safer at school than at home. Should volunteers have to undergo the same background checks as teachers?

Sample Essay

Schools have always sought to involve parents in their children's educations. For most parents that involvement is receiving progress reports and rank cards. Some of them attend open houses or participate in parent/teacher conferences, although those numbers decline as the children leave elementary school, and, by the time they've reached high school, few parents ever cross the thresholds of the schools their children attend. If a child participates in sports or plays in the band, his or her parents may attend games or concerts. Many school and teachers want parents to know what goes on in their schools and classrooms in order to develop transparency. After all, schools aren't- or shouldn't be – trying to hide anything. Today, schools are facing budget cuts that have decimated the ranks of teacher aides who performed tasks that teachers, with their busy schedules, don't have time to do. Custodial staffs are smaller, and schools aren't as clean or well-maintained as they used to be. Volunteerism seems the solution to a number of problems that schools face. However, requiring volunteerism is not a valid concept either in its phrasing or expectations.

Volunteerism by its definition is something done of one's free will; it is a choice. Requiring someone to volunteer changes the entire concept. How does one enforce mandatory volunteerism? What are the consequences for parents who can't or won't volunteer? When a requirement is not met, consequences do ensue. If one doesn't pay his/her taxes, the government levies a fine or sentences the violator to jail. Would schools fine parents who don't volunteer? Maybe they or their child would get detention. Clearly, the enforcement of such a policy would be difficult at best and unfair at worst.

There are bound to be parents who can not, will not, or should not volunteer at their children's schools. It's probably safe to say that most parents work today. How would they fulfill the requirement to volunteer? The recommendation does not specify that the volunteerism must take place during the school day, but should working parents give up time with their families on their days off from work? Just as some children refuse to do their school work, there are parents who will simply refuse to volunteer at their children's schools. They pay their taxes to support the schools in their district, and that should be enough of a contribution. There are parents who, under no circumstance, should be allowed to volunteer at their children's schools. Some parents are physically, psychologically, or sexually abusive. Their children may think of school as an escape from a dangerous home, even if it is only for a few hours of the day. What would the impact be on those children if their parents were to show up in their classrooms on a regular basis?

Adults who work in school systems today, from the principal and teachers to the bus drivers must undergo fingerprinting and background checks before they can work around children. Shouldn't volunteers be subject to the same scrutiny? After all, we are letting them into spaces populated by our most vulnerable citizens. What is the liability to a school system when a volunteer becomes a danger to children? Teachers serve in loco parentis, in the parents' place while their children are at school. Parents trust that their children are safe, and it is the school's responsibility to see that they are.

School systems face a number of challenges today. Administrators and teachers are being asked to do more with less. Volunteerism seems a way to fill some of the needs that are not met by tight budgets. Some wonderful people do give freely of their time and talents to help out in their local schools, but the rewards aren't worth the risks of requiring all parents to volunteer in their children's schools.

Issue Task 21

> *Colleges and universities should require their students to spend at least one semester studying in a foreign country.*
>
> Write a response in which you discuss the extent to which you agree or disagree with the recommendation and explain your reasoning for the position you take. In developing and supporting your position, describe specific circumstances in which adopting the recommendation would or would not be advantageous and explain how these examples shape your position.

Strategies

Restate the Recommendation:

Restate the recommendation by telling what students should not do while retaining the original meaning.

In other words:

Students should not complete college without being required to spend at least one semester studying in a foreign country.

You could also determine what question is being answered by the recommendation.

What should colleges recommend that all of their students do before completing their educations?

Or: *Should colleges recommend that all of their students spend at least one semester studying in a foreign country?*

Creating a question will allow you to think about the way you would answer it and why you would answer it in that way.

Now identify the parts of the recommendation that provide evidence that you can affirm or refute.

a) **require** – This word leaves no room for choice. By the time students are in college, they should be able to make some choices about where they study.

b) **all** – Again, there is no room for compromise. Will all college students benefit from studying abroad? Some fields of study may be enriched by a semester abroad.

Opposing viewpoint:

Colleges and universities should not require all of their students to spend at least one semester studying in a foreign country.

Identify the parts of the opposing recommendation that provide evidence for you to affirm or refute.

a) **require** – As in the original recommendation, this word leaves no room for equivocation. In this case, it is followed by the word not, so the requirement is negated.

b) **all** – This word allows no exceptions. When a statement includes not before all, one may interpret it to mean some. Should some students be required to study abroad?

Alternatives:

Is there another way to look at this issue? Many colleges and universities do have required classes for students seeking degrees in particular majors. Should candidates in some majors be required to study abroad? Would it be a financial hardship for some? Should study abroad simply be an available option for college students? Many colleges and universities make study abroad available for third year.

New viewpoint:

Colleges and universities should make study in a foreign country available to all of its students.

Examples and Reasons:

a) the global economy – A country's economy relies on those of countries around the world. Students in business or economy could benefit from studying those aspects of a foreign country in that country itself.

b) foreign language students – These students would most obviously benefit from studying the language immersed in the culture of the country and living with native speakers of the language.

c) requiring a semester abroad could be a financial hardship for students. Many students have to work their way through college. The likelihood of being able to work in a foreign country is slim.

d) nontraditional students. Most colleges today have a number of nontraditional students. They are older and may be married with children. They may have jobs. Forcing them to study abroad is shortsighted.

e) online colleges

Sample Essay

The chance to earn college credit while studying abroad is an attractive option, and that is what it should remain. The world's shrinking size makes it seem practical to require students to spend at least one semester studying in a foreign country. Most of those students would develop a better understanding of the global perspective, but it simply isn't a practical option for many young people. Colleges and universities must look at the issue from several sides before adopting this requirement.

Students in some programs of study would benefit from study abroad, while for students in other programs, the requirement would be a burden. Those who are studying a foreign language are the most obvious beneficiaries of studying in another country. What better way to learn French, for example, than to immerse oneself in the culture of France. Rubbing shoulders on a daily basis with people whose native tongue is French is the best way to grasp the nuances of the language that are virtually impossible to impart in a classroom setting. Familiarity with the landscape, the food, and the arts of a country impart a depth of understanding that would be difficult to obtain in any other manner. Earning credit while strolling on the Champs Elysees or reading a text book while lounging on the Rive Gauche is similar to earning a bonus at work. As idyllic as this seems, it is a hardship for some students, even those studying foreign languages. College is an enormous financial commitment, and many can't do it without holding down at least one job while attending school. For those who would have to forfeit a job for even a semester, this requirement would be onerous.

Another segment of the college population that might derive a benefit from studying in another country is those who plan to enter the world of finance or economics. No country stands alone in the global economy. Goods are produced and sold across borders every day. Gone are the days of a country producing all of the consumables for its citizens. The American stock and commodities markets fluctuate hourly based on what is happening in markets around the world. For students entering this arena, studying other markets first hand would be more enlightening than reading a textbook about it. These students, however, may get that opportunity after obtaining a job in a multinational organization and visit other countries on someone else's dime. In addition, such opportunities are limited, so some students would likely be placed with a company that has no relation to their preferred career path.

Colleges and universities must consider the nontraditional students on their campuses. No longer are campuses populated only by 18 to 22-year-olds. Women are entering college after raising their children; displaced adult workers are returning to learn new skills; and veterans are taking advantage of college tuition earned while serving their country. Should schools require these students, who have other responsibilities, to leave everything behind and spend a semester in a foreign country?

Finally, one must ask if the emerging online universities should embrace this requirement. Online students are enrolled for the convenience of being able to complete coursework from the comfort of their own homes. Requiring them to study abroad for a semester seems contradictory to the philosophies of these schools. Finishing the traditional course of study is enough of a challenge for most students without the additional burden of living and studying in a foreign country. Universities should, nonetheless, make available the option to spend at least a semester abroad, but this should not be a mandatory requirement.

Issue Task 22

> *People's behavior is largely determined by forces not of their own making.*
>
> Write a response in which you discuss the extent to which you agree or disagree with the claim. In developing and supporting your position, be sure to address the most compelling reasons and/or examples that could be used to challenge your position.

Strategies

Assumptions:

What are the assumptions in the claim? These will be statements that you can either affirm or refute.

Assumption 1: Behavior is influenced by outside forces.

Assumption 2: People can rationalize their behavior.

Assumption 3: There are forces beyond one's control.

Assumption 4: People don't have to take responsibility for their own actions.

Assumption 5: Both good and bad behavior is accidental.

Assumption 6: One's behavior is not deliberate.

Opposing viewpoint:

People's behavior is not determined by outside forces.

What are the assumptions in this claim? As before, they will be statements that you can either affirm or refute.

Assumption 1: People are responsible for their own behavior.

Assumption 2: People can ignore outside forces.

Assumption 3: People's behavior is influenced by something other than outside forces.

Alternative claim:

In some cases, people's behavior is determined by outside forces.

Assumption 1: People's behavior may be influenced by outside forces.

Assumption 2: People's behavior is sometimes beyond their control.

Sample Essay

In the mid 1970's, San Francisco supervisor, Dan White, killed Mayor Moscone and supervisor Harvey Milk. White had become despondent over the actions of the mayor and the homosexual activist, Milk, to change the laws pertaining to homosexual rights in the city. White's lawyer claimed that White's deepening depression led him to eat foods high in sugar, which affected his behavior. One of the reporters during White's trial coined the term, "the Twinkie defense", named for the well-known snack cake. That phrase is resurrected every time a defendant in a particularly heinous crime claims that some circumstance beyond his control made him behave badly. History provides shining examples of when circumstances did not reduce humans to use excuses to behave badly.

In 1944, a teenaged Elie Wiesel, his parents and sisters, were forced from their home in Hungary and transported to the infamous concentration camp, Auschwitz. At the entrance to the camp, this Jewish boy and his father were separated from his mother and sisters. Elie was just fourteen years old at the time, but another man in line told him to lie and say that he was sixteen; otherwise, he would be considered too young to work and would be sent to extermination along with women and children. During the ensuing months, Elie and his father endured harsh living and working conditions and starvation. When his father became ill, he tried to convince Elie to eat his ration of food, but Elie refused to sacrifice his father to ensure his own survival. Even when the prisoners were ordered to abandon the camp ahead of the Allies imminent arrival, Elie did everything he could to see that his father would survive. He watched as other fathers or sons abandoned those who could no longer endure the enforced race throughout the cold and snowy landscape but declined to forsake his own humanity.

History has recorded the deeds of others who, during the Holocaust, chose the high road rather than take the easy way out. Miep Gies, at great risk to herself, hid and supplied provisions to the family of Anne Frank while they hid in an attic in Amsterdam. Oskar Schindler made it possible for Jewish workers in his factory to escape the horrors of the Nazi regime. These heroes could have succumbed to circumstances, and history would likely have excused them. People can be the masters of their own destinies. Neither Twinkies nor "the devils made me do it" are acceptable excuses for relinquishing that mastery.

Issue Task 23

Although innovations such as video, computers, and the Internet seem to offer schools improved methods for instructing students, these technologies all too often distract from real learning.

Write a response in which you discuss the extent to which you agree or disagree with the statement and explain your reasoning for the position you take. In developing and supporting your position, you should consider ways in which the statement might or might not hold true and explain how these considerations shape your position.

Strategies

Restate the Issue:

Begin by restating the issue. Make the dependent clause the main clause of the sentence. Rearranging the clauses changes the focus and the connotation of each clause.

In other words:

Although technology all too often distracts from real learning, innovations such as video, computers, and the Internet seem to offer schools improved methods for instructing students.

Determine the question being answered by the statement.

What effect has technology had on teaching and learning?

The question may start you thinking about the way that you would answer it. Your own position may be taking shape. The question should help develop alternate points of view. The original issue statement is only one way to answer the question.

Now think about parts of the original issue statement that provide evidence you can affirm or refute.

a) **innovations** – The root word, nova, means new. Innovations don't remain innovative for long. At one time, cars, telephones, television, and typewriters were innovative.

b) **seem** – Seem is not a definitive word. It's not an absolute.

c) **to offer** – One does not have to accept an offer. An offer implies choice.

d) **improved** – This implies better, that what came before was not as good in some way.

e) **distract** – This is the opposite of attract. Distract means to lead away from, while attract means to lead toward.

f) **real learning**– Real is the opposite of artificial or fake. Is any learning artificial or fake?

Opposing viewpoint:

Innovations such as video, computer, and the Internet offer schools improved methods for instructing students and promote real learning.

Identify the parts of the opposing statement that provide evidence to refute or affirm.

a) **promote** – Promote means to move forward. Technology helps learning to move forward. You may create a statement that qualifies the original or opposing viewpoint.

Alternative viewpoint:

Innovations such as video, computers, and the Internet have the potential to either offer schools improved methods for instructing students or to distract from real learning.

Identify the parts of the alternative viewpoint that provide evidence to refute or affirm.

a) **potential** – The root of potential is potent, which means having power. Technology has the power to offer school improved methods for instructing students, or it has the power to distract from real learning.

Position:

With appropriate training, teachers and students can use technology such as videos, computers, and the Internet to enhance teaching and learning.

Examples:

a) **Record keeping** – teachers can use web-based grade books to keep track of assignments and student progress. Schools can allow students and parents, access to those grade books, placing responsibility for completing assignments and awareness of problems on the student and parents.

b) **Communication** – Schools and/or individual teachers can create web sites to communicate with students by placing assignments, special directions, etc on the Internet. Teachers and/or schools can communicate with students and parents via email.

c) **Google docs** – web–based application that allows students to create office documents such as slide presentations, spread sheets and compositions. This allows students to submit assignments without printing them; students can collaborate with each other or their teachers; and teachers can leave comments.

d) **Research** – multiple students can research the same topic simultaneously without worrying about books already checked out of the library. Teachers can use anti plagiarism programs.

Sample Essay

In the early part of the twentieth century, people thought the car was a fad; they would never replace the trusty, hard-working horse. In the middle of the twentieth century, people thought television was a fad; it would never replace the radio. In the mid 1980's, people thought VCR's and video tapes were a fad; they would never replace the experience of going to the movies. Now we can drive in our cars and watch movies at the same time. Virtually everything that makes life more convenient will stay. We must accept that technology in the form of computers and the Internet are permanently entrenched in society.

What is the impact on teaching and learning? Teaching and learning has always been book and paper intensive. Teachers in every discipline assigned books to their students and used paper to keep track of which student had which book. Students used paper to complete assignments associated with those books and handed them in to their teachers, who carried those papers home to grade them. This process was repeated all over the country by millions of students and teachers every day for 36 -40 weeks a year. Technology has the potential to allow students to complete a variety of work and submit it online.

Most notable of these applications is Google docs where students can set up a free account and create writing pieces, spreadsheets, and slide presentations. Alternatively, they can upload those same documents from their home computers. Students share their work with their teachers who can insert comments, highlight elements, and assign grades. In fact, a student and teacher can work simultaneously on an assignment while "chatting" in a side bar. Another benefit of Google docs is the feature that saves a student's work instantaneously and keeps it on the Web. This application enhances the educational process through its accessibility and immediacy. When teachers can provide rapid feedback, students benefit.

Technology is s double-edged sword when it comes to research projects. On one side, information on any topic is available at the click of a mouse. On the other side is the temptation for students to cut and paste information directly from sources. There have always been students who plagiarize. Technology can make it easier, but it also is easier for teachers to uncover it using programs designed for that purpose or simply using Google's search function. Thanks to the Internet, gone are the days of creating Works Cited or References pages by hand and agonizing over alphabetizing and citing correctly. There are both free and subscription services that can do that for students. When students and teachers can focus on what the child has to say and how he says it, real learning happens.

The introduction of tablets is already revolutionizing learning. It is likely that future students will not be carrying backpacks crammed with book and binders. Rather, they will glide from class to class carrying slim computer onto which they have downloaded their textbooks, and with which they will complete their classwork. As the accouterments of education become easier to manage, there can be a clearer focus on leveraging these new technologies to better educate students. Therefore, while technology has the potential to distract students from learning if used poorly, its true potential lies in its ability to streamline classroom work and homework, giving students more time to learn about topics that may not have been covered otherwise.

Issue Task 24

> *The best ideas arise from a passionate interest in commonplace things.*
>
> Write a response in which you discuss the extent to which you agree or disagree with the statement and explain your reasoning for the position you take. In developing and supporting your position, you should consider ways in which the statement might or might not hold true and explain how these considerations shape your position.

Strategies

Restate the Issue:

In this case, you might invert the order of the ideas.

In other words:

A passionate interest in commonplace things gives rise to the best ideas.

Or: *It is not an interest in the uncommon that gives rise to the best ideas.*

You might determine what question is being answered by the issue statement.

From what do the best ideas arise?

Or: *Where do the best ideas come from?*

Creating a question may help you to formulate your own position on the issue and help you decide how strongly you agree or disagree with it.

Now think about the parts of the statement that provide evidence that you can affirm or refute.

    a) **best** – This is the superlative form of good. It doesn't get any better.

    b) **ideas** – Why not products or inventions? Are ideas themselves worth much unless they are the basis of a useful product or invention?

    c) **passionate** – This is a strong word. It carries more weight than a passing interest would.

    d) **commonplace** – A synonym is everyday. Is it likely that most people take notice of everyday or commonplace things?

Opposing viewpoint:

The best ideas arise from a passionate interest in unusual things.

Identify the parts of the opposing statement that provide evidence for you to refute or affirm.

    a) **unusual** – This is the opposite of commonplace. Unusual means not usual or common or everyday.

Alternatives

Is there any other way to look at this issue? Perhaps it is not the things themselves that inspire, but the actions of the things in consideration.

New viewpoint:

The best ideas arise from a passionate interest in the behavior of commonplace things.

    a)   **behavior** – The way things act may be the inspiration for new ideas.

Examples and reasons:

    a)   Observing the changes of the stars in the night sky being used for navigation.

    b)   Man's desire to fly like birds.

Sample Essay

One tends to think of visionaries as men and women who can see things that the minds of mere mortals cannot even imagine. Modern conveniences like the telephone and the television seem like miracles. How can a camera take a moving picture on the other side of the world and send it to the television in my little corner of the world? How is it possible that my voice can travel into space and be retrieved by my friend on her phone in the middle of the country? These inventions are ultimately based on commonplace ideas and actions, such as looking up at a full moon as a child and wondering what it would be like to be there. Many wonders of the modern world do have their roots in objects that we observe every day.

Man has always envied birds. The desire to fly has given rise to myths as old as the ability of man to speak. The most familiar of these myths is populated by the master craftsman, Daedalus and his son, Icarus. Icarus' desire to fly led his father to craft wings made of feather and wax. Daedalus' copied what he could observe of the wings of birds. His only warning to his son was not to fly too close to the sun lest the wax melt and cause the wings to be destroyed. Icarus, enthralled by the freedom of flight, ignored his father's warning and soared higher and higher until he did, indeed, flies too close to the sun. The wax melted, the wings fell apart, and Icarus' plummeted to his death in the sea. In the fifteenth century, Leonardo da Vinci drew plans for a flying device that became the inspiration for the modern helicopter. Some of the earliest planes attempted to imitate the motion of birds' wings. Now that man can actually fly not only around the world but out of it, one must wonder, "Do the birds envy man."

As the birds move in the sky above us, so do the sun, the stars, and the moon. For much of the history of man, the stars and planets were sources of myth and inspired poets, artists and musicians. The earliest ideas about the sun and the stars made the Earth the center of the universe. Later astronomers created the heliocentric theory of our solar system. The first practical use of the stars was for navigation. The longer the scientists observed the heavenly bodies, the greater the desire grew to reach them. When it became possible to measure the distances to the sun, the moon, and other planets, the idea of reaching them became a possibility. Now man has been to the moon, and has set his sights on Mars. The Hubble telescope continues to send back crystal-clear pictures of deep space, and man's fascination continues to grow.

When man looks up, he cannot avoid seeing the birds and the heavenly bodies. They are ubiquitous, and man's envy, fascination, and eventual understanding of them have made incredible journeys possible. The best ideas of the future are likely to come from man's continued passion for commonplace things.

Issue Task 25

> *To be an effective leader, a public official must maintain the highest ethical and moral standards.*
>
> Write a response in which you discuss the extent to which you agree or disagree with the claim. In developing and supporting your position, be sure to address the most compelling reasons and/or examples that could be used to challenge your position.

Strategies

Assumptions:

What are the assumptions in the claim?

Assumption 1: Ethics and morals determine effectiveness.

Assumption 2: Ethical and moral standards of leaders must be higher than those of average people.

Assumption 3: Leaders are held to a higher standard that the average person.

Assumption 4: Ethical and moral standards are easily defined and constant everywhere.

Assumption 5: Leaders outside of the public arena do not need to meet the same standards as those who are in the public arena.

Assumption 6: Ethics and morals are essentially the same part of someone's character. Can one be ethical while being immoral?

Opposing viewpoint:

A public figure does not have to maintain the highest ethical and moral standards to be an effective leader.

Assumption 1: A leader's effectiveness depends on elements other than high ethical and moral standards.

Alternative claim:

As long as it doesn't affect his service to the people, a public official should be held to standards no higher than those of the rest of society.

Assumption 1: A public official's private behavior should not necessarily be used to judge his effectiveness as a leader.

Assumption 2: Public officials can separate their private lives from their public ones.

Support for alternative claim

Example: President Franklin Delano Roosevelt kept a mistress. Did this detract from his ability to lead American out of the Great Depression?

Example: Adolph Hitler was supremely successful as a leader despite his lack of ethics and morals.

Example: J. Edgar Hoover, director of the FBI, was a cross dresser.

Sample Essay

Are morals and ethics the same thing? Can one behave ethically in business, medicine, or politics while exhibiting immoral behavior in private? Numerous examples throughout history portray the effectiveness of leaders who displayed, either publicly or privately, behaviors or beliefs that would be considered unethical or immoral. If the constituencies of a public official are being well-served, do they care about the private behavior of those officials? When the public good is being served, the public is likely to be satisfied and willing to disregard other parts of an official's life.

History has declared Franklin Delano Roosevelt to have been a supremely effective leader of the United States of American through some its darkest days despite the fact that he had a long-time mistress. Unprecedented in the history of the US is Roosevelt's election to four consecutive terms in the White House. He must have been doing something right. Taking office at the height of the Great Depression, FDR, himself a child of privilege, began to demand of Congress that they institute programs that would lead to the nation's recovery. The New Deal was born and spawned such programs as the Civilian Conservation Corps, the Tennessee Valley Authority, and the Works Progress Administration. All of these provided jobs for Americans who otherwise would have spent their days standing in bread lines or sleeping on the streets. On Sunday, December 7, 1941, the Japanese attacked the American military fleet at Pearl Harbor, and FDR had to make the painful decision to declare war against Japan. Although FDR did not live to see the atomic bombs dropped on Hiroshima or Nagasaki, the US was the eventual victor in the war that he had declared. The fact that he was with his mistress when he died in Warm Springs, Georgia, did not stop Americans from lining up by the thousands to watch the train carrying his body back to Washington, D.C. The citizens' interests had been served and preserved by this great man, and that was what mattered to them.

Despite his obvious lack of morals, Adolph Hitler is recognized as an effective leader. A contemporary of FDR's, he rose to power when Germany was suffering economically because of the reparations laid on the country after WWI, as well as the Great Depression. Hitler's promise to lift Germany out of the economic quagmire attracted the votes of the German people, and Hitler became Chancellor of Germany. His efforts to recoup Germany's losses included invading nearby countries. He also sought to punish those he felt responsible for Germany's downfall, namely Jewish bankers and businessmen, who, in his mind, had far too much control of the finances of Europe. Because their welfare was secure, the citizens of Germany lived and worked in towns next to concentration camps in which Jews, Catholics, homosexuals and the mentally feeble were systematically being exterminated and claimed that they didn't know what was taking place. Using immoral and unethical means, Hitler served the interests of a subset of the German people, and that was what mattered to them.

It has been said that a group eventually gets the leadership it deserves. Whether the leader is upright and moral or unethical and immoral may depend on the character of the people who elect him/her. It just may be that, if the standards are too high, men and women who, otherwise, would be effective leaders, will not seek to lead.

Issue Task 26

> *Critical judgment of work in any given field has little value unless it comes from someone who is an expert in that field.*
>
> Write a response in which you discuss the extent to which you agree or disagree with the claim. In developing and supporting your position, be sure to address the most compelling reasons and/or examples that could be used to challenge your position.

Strategies

Assumptions:

Identify the assumptions in the claim. These will be statements that you can either affirm or refute.

Assumption 1: Only experts in a field are competent to critique or judge work in that field.

Assumption 2: Every field has an expert.

Opposing viewpoint:

It is possible to provide critical judgment of work in a given field even if one is not an expert in the field.

What are the assumptions in this claim?

Assumption 1: All critical judgment is valuable.

Assumption 2: One need not be an expert to judge the value of work in a given field.

Is there another way of looking at this claim? Why might someone make this claim? What is the claim trying to prove or disprove? Begin a dependent clause with the word, although, and follow it with the claim.

Although consumers of technology express opinions about the products, critical judgment. There are a variety of choices, but whatever you choose can help you formulate your position and develop your response.

Sample Essay

To claim that the only valid judgment of a product that is the result of work in some field can arise from an expert in that field neglects the users or consumers of that product. The purpose of developing a new theory or designing a new object is, at its core, to be used by others. All work requires feedback to be either validated or improved, and this feedback should come from both experts in the field and people whose lives will be impacted by it.

At the most esoteric level, the claim can refer to scientific or mathematical theory. Perhaps the only qualified critics are other scientists or mathematicians. However, the practical application of the theories may include products intended for use by laymen. The first product that comes to mind is the personal computer. That the computing devices we use today evolved from ENIAC, a computer that filled two large rooms and could only complete mathematical computations, is almost beyond belief. It seemed for awhile that the computer would remain the province of science and mathematics, and any improvements or advances in computing would be self-serving. Once computers became small enough and reasonably priced, they became available to the average person. Consumers were enthralled. Once they mastered the functions possible on those early machines, they wanted - even demanded - more. The industry responded. The average consumer may not know how a computer works, but they know what they want it to do. As brilliant as computer scientists may be, they might not be able to imagine what the average Joe wants or needs. Even without computer science expertise, a consumer who uses their computer to shop online or search for recipes has had an impact on the industry.

At a more approachable level are contemporary writers. When a new novel is published, the phrase, critically acclaimed, should signal soaring success for the author. Some authors, in fact, are satisfied with critical approbation. It may not, however, herald financial rewards. If the purpose of writing is to be read, the inexpert public's opinion may be more valuable than the critics'. If Stephen King, probably the best-selling author in the last forty years, had listened to the experts in his field, he would have stopped writing after Carrie was published. Instead, he listened to his own muse and turned out thrillers that have his readers clamoring for more.

On an even more mundane level are the household appliances that are intended to make life easier. Without the input of consumers, the wringer washer might still be the latest technology in laundry help. Customers would still be hanging rugs outside and using a paddle to beat the dirt out of them. The average person may not understand the technology involved in designing time-saving appliances, but they are experts in their use.

To say that critical judgment has little value unless the judgment comes from experts depends on the purpose of the work and the intended audience. If something is accomplished for purely scientific reasons, the only critical judgment of value may be that of experts in the field. If one produces something for public consumption, he or she should not only expect, but welcome the public's opinion.

Issue Task 27

> *Claim: The surest indicator of a great nation is not the achievements of its rulers, artists, or scientists.*
>
> *Reason: The surest indicator of a great nation is actually the welfare of all its people.*
>
> Write a response in which you discuss the extent to which you agree or disagree with the claim and the reason on which that claim is based.

NOTE: *The above topic has wording similar to Issue Task 4 of GRE Analytical Writing Solution to the Real Essay Topics - Book 1. However, if you read carefully you will notice that the task instructions are different. Hence, it is very important to read the topic as well as its instructions completely before you start to write your response.*

Strategies

Restate the Claim:

Combine the claim and reason into a single statement.

In other words:

The surest indicator of a great nation is actually the welfare of all its people rather than the achievements of its rulers, artists, or scientists.

What are the assumptions in the claim and reason? These will be statements that you can wither affirm or refute in your response.

Assumption 1: The achievements of rulers, artists, or scientists are not a nation's most important achievements.

Assumption 2: People judge a nation's success by the achievement of its rulers, artists, or scientists.

Assumption 3: The welfare of its people is the most important accomplishment of any nation.

Assumption 4: The achievements of a nation's rulers, artists, or scientists do not contribute to the welfare of its people.

Next, create a statement that expresses the opposing point of view, using language similar to that in the original claim. In this case, the reason could become the claim, and the claim becomes the reason.

Opposing viewpoint:

Claim – The surest indicator of a great nation is not the welfare of all of its people.

Reason – The surest indicator of a great nation is the achievements of its rulers, artists or scientists.

How does this new claim and reason affect the earlier assumptions?

Assumption 1: The accomplishments of a nation's rulers, artists, or scientists determine a nation's greatness.

Assumption 2: The welfare of a country's people does not determine the greatness of that nation.

Assumption 3: Outsiders judge a nation by the accomplishments of its rulers, artists, or scientists.

Alternative claim:

An important indicator of a nation's greatness is the achievements of its rulers, artists, or scientists.

Alternative reason:

The welfare of a nation's people depends on those achievements.

Assumption 1: A country is judged by the achievements of its rulers, artists, or scientists.

Assumption 2: The achievements of a nation's rulers, artists, or scientists affect the welfare of its people.

Support for alternative claim and reason:

Example 1: The achievements of Abraham Lincoln had a profound effect on the welfare of all Americans. The Civil War reunited the states. The Emancipation Proclamation freed the slaves.

Example 2: The Human Genome Project has enabled doctors and scientists to isolate genes responsible for deadly diseases.

Example 3: Adolph Hitler and Joseph Mengele performed atrocities upon specific populations in Europe during the 1930's and 1940's.

Sample Essay

It is nearly impossible to separate the welfare of a nation's population from the achievements of that nation's rulers, scientists, or artists. Whether the citizens' welfare is enhanced or diminished depends on the type and scope of those achievements. History is replete with examples of rulers who made history-changing decisions, of scientists whose research and experiments altered the lives of millions, and of artists whose words or images affected the thinking of a nation's citizenry. As these two ideas are so thoroughly intertwined in each other, the surest indicator of a great (or poor) nation is a combination of the welfare of the population and the achievements of its leaders.

The welfare of every American was affected by decisions that Abraham Lincoln made during his presidency in the nineteenth century. His belief that a nation divided cannot stand led to the decision to declare war on the Confederate states and an eventual reunification of the states of the United States. During the Civil War, Lincoln issued the Emancipation Proclamation intended to free the slaves. That proclamation had both immediate and long-range effects. Although discrimination still exists in America, the descendents of those freed slaves have more opportunities than their ancestors. Martin Luther King, Jr, in the middle of the twentieth century, led the struggle to validate the meaning of the Emancipation Proclamation and brought change for all disenfranchised groups in the country.

Perhaps the most reviled leader of the twentieth century is Adolph Hitler. Der Fuhrer's achievements led to the near eradication of an entire religious group in eastern Europe. His insidious actions forced millions of Jews to leave their homes and businesses to live in ghettos and, eventually in relocation or concentration camps where they were systematically killed through overwork, starvation, and disease. Dr. Joseph Mengele conducted medical experiments on that same group of people with the ostensible goal of serving humanity. Nobody, apart from Megele himself, derived any benefit from his actions. The only tangible artistic accomplishment during Hitler's reign was the theft of great works of art from the countries that Germany occupied.

In the world of the present, the actions of one nation's ruler, scientists, or artists can influence the welfare of people in many nations. The world has grown small. The butterfly effect can apply to any action. If a child in Africa dies from the AIDS virus, it is a signal to the entire world that effective treatment of the disease is still not widely available, and the cry goes out to governments and drug companies to act. If a terrorist in Japan releases deadly Sarin in a subway station, the rest of the world goes on alert. If Muslim extremists fly passenger planes into the tallest buildings in the United States, reprisals against people of Middle Eastern descent are carried out in small towns and cities around the world. Whether rulers make the decision to declare war on terrorism, or scientists develop better antidotes for deadly poisons, or artists create depictions of the horrors of violent death, the welfare of people in all countries is affected in ways that may not be demonstrated for years or decades.

The welfare of a nation's citizens is irrevocably tied to the achievements of its rulers, artists, and scientists. The standard of living, excellence of education, accessibility to quality health care, and feelings of security in any nation reflect decisions made by its rulers, advances accomplished by its scientists, and representations of the culture depicted in the words and images of its artists. History serves as the final judge of the eras in which those events occurred.

Issue Task 28

> *When old buildings stand on ground that modern planners feel could be better used for modern purposes, modern development should be given precedence over the preservation of historic buildings.*
>
> Write a response in which you discuss the extent to which you agree or disagree with the statement and explain your reasoning for the position you take. In developing and supporting your position, you should consider ways in which the statement might or might not hold true and explain how these considerations shape your position.

Strategies

Restate the Issue:

In this case, you might reverse the order in which the parts of the issue appear and use a negative phrase.

In other words:

The preservation of historic buildings should not be given precedence over using the ground they stand on for modern purposes that have a better use.

You could also determine what question is being answered by the statement.

Should the preservation of historic buildings be given precedence over modern development?

Asking a question may help you to formulate your response to the issue.

Now think about the parts of the statement that provide evidence that you can affirm or refute.

a) **old** – This implies outdated or rundown. New is better.

b) **better used** – better is a comparative word. It is more than good but less than best.

c) **modern purposes** – Modern implies improved. It is the opposite of old fashioned.

d) **development** – This word also has a positive connotation. It implies improvement, evolution.

e) **precedence** – Whatever is being proposed is more important than other ideas. It should come ahead of other plans or ideas.

f) **preservation** – Again, the connotation is positive. To preserve is to save.

g) **historic** – Something historic is a representation of history. One generally thinks favorably of something that is described as being historic.

Opposing viewpoint:

Modern development should not be given precedence over the preservation of historic buildings that stand on ground, which modern planners feel could be better used for modern purposes.

The only new evidence in the opposing statement is the word not, which simply reverses the original position.

Alternatives

Is there any other way to look at this issue? Can you qualify either of the statements? Are there any cases where one or the other of the statements might be true or not true?

New viewpoint:

When the preservation of historic buildings becomes a financial struggle or the land on which they stand could be used for community betterment, modern development should be given precedence over that preservation.

Identify parts of the new viewpoint that provide evidence for you to refute or affirm.

   a) **financial struggle** – Surely communities and special interest groups cannot afford to preserve every building of an historic value.

   b) **community betterment**– This is subjective. What one feels is betterment, another might feel is a detriment to the community. Who decides?

Examples:

   a) Auschwitz is crumbling. There is strong debate over preserving what remains of the infamous Nazi concentration camp or the suitability of letting the buildings crumble. Is there a better use for this land?

   b) Urban renewal generally involves tearing down existing structures to make way for improved buildings to house new business or offices or to improve traffic flow.

Sample Essay

The value of any object is subjective. Nostalgia for the simpler life of bygone days causes us to attach more value than appropriate to objects from the past. Historic buildings let us envision the people who lived in them and the daily activities they pursued. However, the needs of communities have changed, and sentiment may need to be discarded to meet those needs. Due to this fact, historic buildings may need to be taken down or otherwise changed to accommodate the needs of the current population.

Some cities have found ways to preserve historic buildings by erecting the new ones over them. Their front walls become part of the new facade. The cities' needs for more office space or apartments have been met and a record of the past has been saved for present and future generations. Many communities in the United States have historical societies who raise money for historic preservation, and, in some cases, old buildings can be listed in the Register of Historic Places and are supported by public funds. The future of projects like these depends on continued interest, and emerging generations may have different priorities.

How essential are old buildings in maintaining the character of a place? When one looks at several cities in Europe, he sees a cityscape very different from the one that existed prior to WWII when both Allies and Axis bombs destroyed ancient structures. The citizens of those towns and cities had no choice but to rebuild. Life went on. Currently, there is debate about the future of Auschwitz. What remains of the notorious Nazi concentration camp is in disrepair. Buildings that were not built to last in the first place are crumbling. Maintaining them is costly. Although many countries around the world have donated millions to the preservation of the site, some wonder if allowing the site return to its pre-WWII state is a more fitting memorial to what happened there. Could the money needed to restore the barracks, the crematoria and to maintain the museum be used in a more appropriate way to teach future generations about the dangers of hatred and prejudice?

Modern technology has made the preservation of old buildings and landmarks possible through photographs and video recordings. In fact, it is possible, with the click of a computer mouse, to take virtual tours of places one has never physically visited. These photos and videos live on the World Wide Web forever, and maintenance costs will be minimal. Access to these historic buildings is no longer restricted to those who can make the trip to their physical sites but is available to anyone with an Internet connection.

Change for the sake of change is frivolous and usually unnecessary, but towns and cities are challenged to make the best use of the spaces they have. Their needs have changed. A small city may need assisted living quarters for its senior citizens or recreational facilities for its young people. To accomplish that, city planners may have to make difficult choices, some of which could include the razing of old buildings.

Issue Task 29

> *Claim: Knowing about the past cannot help people to make important decisions today.*
>
> *Reason: The world today is significantly more complex than it was even in the relatively recent past.*
>
> Write a response in which you discuss the extent to which you agree or disagree with the claim and the reason on which that claim is based.

NOTE: *The above topic has wording similar to Issue Task 14 of GRE Analytical Writing Solution to the Real Essay Topics - Book 2. However, if you read carefully you will notice that the task instructions are different. Hence, it is very important to read the topic as well as its instructions completely before you start to write your response.*

Strategies

Combine the claim and the reason into one statement using a subordinate clause.

In other words:

Because the world today is significantly more complex than it was even in the relatively recent past, knowing about the past cannot help people to make important decisions today.

What are the assumptions stated or implied in the claim and reason? These will provide evidence that you can refute or affirm in your argument.

a)   People cannot use their own or others' past experiences to help them make decisions today.

b)   The complexity of today's world makes past events and/or actions irrelevant in the decision-making process.

c)   The complexity of today's society contributes to the difficulty of making decisions.

Opposing viewpoint:

Claim: Knowing about the past does help people make important decisions today.

Reason: The complexity of today's world is no more challenging than that of previous eras.

What are the assumptions stated or implied in the claim and reason? These will provide evidence that you can refute or affirm in your argument.

Assumptions:

a)   The past can inform the present.

b)   Each time period is more complex than the one that preceded it.

c)   The degree of complexity is relative.

Sample Essay

The world today may be more complex than that of the past, but people's needs and motivations have not changed. People make decisions that they think will benefit them in some way. According the Maslow's Hierarchy of Needs, all people desire the same things. They want their physiological needs met; they require food, water, sex, and sleep. They want to feel loved and safe. They desire self esteem and the respect of others. Most humans make decisions to satisfy these needs, and they make use of their own or others' experiences to help them. This lack of change refutes the claim, in that it shows that the past is necessary to make new decisions even with the fast pace of our current world, because history can be used to inform correct decisions based on similar past situations.

My grandparents are in their late eighties; they were born in the 1920's. In the eighty-plus years since their births, they have seen enormous and increasingly rapid changes occur in virtually every aspect of life. They have seen the advent of commercial flight, the construction of the interstate highway system, the invention of television, and the dominance of the computer in twenty-first century living. The first challenges they faced occurred when they were children during the Great Depression. They have used those experiences to inform most of the decisions they have made throughout their lives. Coming from childhoods of financial struggle, they don't waste anything. My grandmother saves used tinfoil and washes and reuses Ziploc bags. My grandfather holds onto even the smallest scrap of lumber from a construction project. He wears his clothes until they are entirely worn out. Whether the economy is good or bad, they manage because their past experiences have taught them the lessons that help them survive and thrive. The complexity of today's world has little effect on them. They make decisions based on their needs and habits.

President Obama is facing some difficult choices concerning Syria's use of chemical weapons against its own citizens. He has tempered his first instinct to initiate an air strike by considering how Americans feel about entering another conflict. When President George W. Bush reacted to the terrorist attack of 9/11/01 by sending troops into Iraq and Afghanistan, he had the support of most Americans. Twelve years later, Americans are weary of these wars and the great majority is not in favor of any more military action. Based on this twelve-year history of American troops in the Middle East, the President has delayed an air strike and is awaiting results of Russia's offer to help Syria dispose of its chemical weapons. Because the world is more complex, President Obama must keep in mind America's recent past before making a decision that can have far-reaching effects. Failure to act against Syria may give other hostile countries the impetus to stockpile chemical weapons. Calling an air strike may cause retaliation against American troops abroad. His primary concern is the safety of Americans, and he uses his knowledge of the past to inform his decisions.

Last fall, the eastern seaboard was hit by super storm Sandy. Lacking sufficient protection from the Atlantic Ocean, seaside resorts and amusement parks in New Jersey were destroyed, and downtown New York City was flooded. Both numerous lives and livelihoods were lost. The island of Manhattan was immobilized as subway tunnels filled with seawater and electricity was lost. Historically, this region did not experience such severe storms, so one could argue that looking to the past for guidance was unwise. However, based on this recent event, city planners are considering the construction of some sort of barrier that would prevent the ocean from entering New York Harbor in the event of another catastrophic storm. Ocean barriers have been used with success in the low countries of Europe, and New York City planners can use the historical success of these countries to help them make important decisions today.

The inherent complexity of living in today's world creates more complexity in the decision-making process. However, it does not preclude using the past as a reference for considering the consequences of those decisions. The world has changed, but its residents have the same needs as those in decades and centuries past, making the criteria for choosing a course of action similar to any in history.

Issue Task 30

> *The best way to understand the character of a society is to examine the character of the men and women that the society chooses as its heroes or its role models.*
>
> Write a response in which you discuss the extent to which you agree or disagree with the claim. In developing and supporting your position, be sure to address the most compelling reasons and/or examples that could be used to challenge your position.

Strategies

Restate the Issue:

In this case, try inverting the clauses.

In other words:

Examining the character of the men and women that the society chooses as its heroes or its role models is the best way to understand the character of that society.

You could also determine what question is being answered by the issue statement.

What is the best way to understand the character of a society?

Or: *What is revealed about a society by examining the character of the men and women that the society chooses as its heroes or its role models?*

Considering how you would answer one or both of the questions may help you to decide to what degree you agree with the original issue statement.

Now think about the part of the original statement that provides evidence that you can affirm or refute.

a) **best way** – Best is the superlative form of good. Any other way would be inferior or produce unsatisfactory results.

b) **understand** – To understand does not mean to validate or agree with an idea. Does examination of the character of a nation's heroes lead to understanding the society? Is this information just one part of a country's character?

c) **character of a society** – Character implies the breadth of morality displayed by a society. It can be negative or positive, strong or weak.

d) **examine** – An examination involves close scrutiny. It means holding something under a microscope to view its smallest parts and then determining how those parts affect or fit into the whole.

e) **chooses** – Choice implies free will. Does every society allow its men and women to choose their heroes and role models? What about countries that have dictatorships or autocracies?

f) **heroes or its role models** – Listing them separately suggests that role models are not necessarily heroes and vice versa. Can someone act heroically and still have attributes that would not make him or her suitable role model? Does heroism depend on special circumstances?

Opposing viewpoint:

Examining the character of the men and women that the society chooses as its heroes or its role models is not the best way to understand the character of that society.

Identify the parts of the opposing statement that provide evidence to affirm or refute. In this case, the only difference is the word, not.

a) **not** – This can be read in two ways. On one hand, it could mean that one should avoid examining the character of the men and women that the society chooses as its heroes or its role models. On the other hand, the statement could imply that this is not the best way or the only way to understand the character of a society.

Alternatives

Is there any other way to look at this issue? Can you qualify the original statement in some way? Is it partially true? Do heroes and role models remain constant? Do they carry over from generation to generation?

New viewpoint:

One way to understand the character of a society is to examine the character of the men and women that the society chooses as its heroes or its role models.

Or: *Because heroes and role models are temporary, the character of a society based on its choice of heroes and role models can only be understood for a specific period in its history.*

Identify the parts of the alternate viewpoint that provide evidence to affirm or refute.

a) **temporary** – People are fickle. Whom they consider to be heroes and role models today may not be the same as those they select tomorrow.

b) **specific period in its history** – Events conspire to create heroes and role models. As the events change, so do the heroes and role models that arise from them.

Position:

Because heroes and role models are temporary, the character of a society based on its choice of heroes and role models can only be understood for a specific period in its history.

Examples and Reasons

a) **President Obama** – His stature as a hero and/or role model has changed since he first decided to run for office.

b) **Charles Barkley** – One-time bad boy of the NBA who said, "I am not a role model."

Sample Essay

Cultures throughout history have been analyzed based on the artifacts they left behind, including architecture, art, writing, household items, and clothing. Archeologists have been able to extrapolate information about a culture's government, scientific knowledge, standard of living, diet, and cosmology. Burial mounds, pyramids, and cave drawings reveal the relative importance of and reverence accorded to individuals in the cultures that produced them. When history began to be recorded in a more systematic manner, writers left records of those who became heroes and role models. Those heroes and role models certainly influenced their cultures, from fashion to morals. That influence, however, was fleeting, and it was not long before someone new became the "flavor of the month". In fact, it may have been the events in history that influenced which men and women were elevated to the status of heroes and role models. The rapid pace of change today makes it nearly impossible to analyze a culture's character based on who is selected to represent the ideal for, as Andy Warhol is credited with saying, everyone will enjoy fifteen minutes of fame.

Charles Barkley, former NBA bad boy, said, "I am not a role model." Professional athletes have often been held to higher standards than people in the general population because of their visibility and high salaries. The paradigm for athletes has always been clean-cut, upstanding, and ethically superior. Before media coverage of every athlete's action became so pervasive, it is likely that those athletes did not always behave well in private or in public, but nobody knew about their bad acts. Parent held athletes up as examples of the kinds of people they wanted their children to become. After all, to reach the ranks of the pros, athletes had to be dedicated to their sport. Children were led to believe that, if they adopted the work ethic and character of professional athletes, they, too, could become supremely successful. When Americans discovered that professional athletes have feet of clay, there was a huge outcry. Charles Barkley's statement was followed by his declaring that parents should be role models for their children. That works well for children whose parents do set a good example, but to whom do the others turn for lessons in good character? Certainly, not to Tiger Woods, whose string of infidelities led to pain and embarrassment for his family, nor to Ron Artest, who engaged in a brawl with a fan during a basketball game.

When the people of the United States became disenchanted with the direction that government was taking during the most recent Bush administration, a young senator from Illinois took up the challenge to lead this country using the mantra of change. Barack Obama declared, "We can do it!" Since his election, the global economy has become precarious, and people in the US are unemployed and losing their homes to foreclosure. Citizens, once filled with hope for the future at the hands of this new president, have become disillusioned, and Barack Obama is no longer seen as the hero they hoped he would be. Basing the character of the United States on the promises made by its presidential candidates is therefore clearly a poor metric, as these candidates do not truly know what kind of change they will be able to effect as President until they are elected into office. Additionally, candidates are likely to paint a picture of an idealized society during their campaigns, which may not reflect the current state of the society at the time.

What are more likely subjects of analysis to determine the character of a society are those institutions or ideas that are more permanent. Rather than looking at the people who have temporarily held the position of hero or role model, look at the form of government that has served a population. Read its constitution. Do they allow the fair and equal treatment of a nation's citizenry? Are punishment and reward meted out in equal measure to citizens of all races, colors, creeds, and genders? The thread that runs through the history of a culture is a better indicator of that culture's character.

Chapter **4**

Analyze an Argument Task

In the Analyze an Argument task, you will take an approach that differs from that in the Analyze an Issue task. You will not be asked to develop and defend a point of view. You will be asked to analyze an argument and the evidence and assumptions on which it is based. You will be presented by a brief passage that makes an argument either for taking some course of action, following a recommendation, or supporting a prediction. You should read the passage carefully to identify either stated or unstated assumptions or to determine the line of reasoning used by the author of the passage. The directions will instruct you to approach your analysis in any of several ways. You may be asked to state what additional evidence is needed to make the argument sound, what questions will need to be answered before accepting a recommendation, or whether a prediction based on the argument is reasonable.

As in the Analyze an Issue task, there is no "right" answer or approach. It is important to stay on topic, use sound reasoning and examples in your response, and strive to develop a coherent, cohesive, and fluent response. Remember that analysis is the act of breaking something down into its components to see how well they relate to each other. The components of the argument may include facts, statistics or other figures, and both stated and unstated assumptions. For example, the owner of Gemma's Jewelry store may predict that, based on the past two years' sales, the store will see an increase of 10% in next year's sales. One of the unstated assumptions is that the demand for luxury goods will increase despite whatever else may happen to the economy. Gemma's Jewelry doesn't say what will account for the increase in sales. Will the store add new lines of merchandise? Will the store increase its advertising? Will the store expand in size? Is a 10% increase significant? If sales were $40,000 last year, is an additional $4,000 dollars in sales meaningful?

You will not need knowledge in any specific discipline to analyze an argument. The topics are of general interest and are accessible to anyone regardless of previous course work. The GRE essay readers will be looking for your ability to reason and organize your thoughts in a logical way. The scoring guide that follows is reprinted from the *Practice Book for the GRE Revised General Test*, developed by Educational Testing Service.

Scoring Guide

Score 6

In addressing the specific task directions, a 6 response presents a cogent, well-articulated analysis of the issue and conveys meaning skillfully.

A typical response in this category:

a)   articulates a clear and insightful position on the issue in accordance with the assigned task

b)   develops the position fully with compelling reasons and/or persuasive examples

c)   sustains a well-focused, well-organized analysis, connecting ideas logically

d)   conveys ideas fluently and precisely, using effective vocabulary and sentence variety

e)   demonstrates facility with the conventions of standard written English (i.e., grammar, usage and mechanics), but may have minor errors

Score 5

In addressing the specific task directions, a 5 response presents a generally thoughtful, well-developed analysis of the issue and conveys meaning clearly.

A typical response in this category:

a)   presents a clear and well-considered position on the issue in accordance with the assigned task

b)   develops the position with logically sound reasons and/or well-chosen examples

c)   is focused and generally well organized, connecting ideas appropriately

d)   conveys ideas clearly and well, using appropriate vocabulary and sentence variety

e)   demonstrates facility with the conventions of standard written English but may have minor errors

Score 4

In addressing the specific task directions, a 4 response presents a competent analysis of the issue and conveys meaning with acceptable clarity.

A typical response in this category:

a)   presents a clear position on the issue in accordance with the assigned task

b)   develops the position with relevant reasons and/or examples

c)   is adequately focused and organized

d)   demonstrates sufficient control of language to express ideas with reasonable clarity

e)   generally demonstrates control of the conventions of standard written English but may have some errors

Score 3

A three response demonstrates some competence in addressing the specific task directions, in analyzing the issue and in conveying meaning, but is obviously flawed.

A typical response in this category exhibits ONE OR MORE of the following characteristics:

a) is vague or limited in addressing the specific task directions and/or in presenting or developing a position on the issue

b) is weak in the use of relevant reasons or examples or relies largely on unsupported claims

c) is poorly focused and/or poorly organized

d) has problems in language and sentence structure that result in a lack of clarity

e) contains occasional major errors or frequent minor errors in grammar, usage or mechanics that can interfere with meaning

Score 2

A two response largely disregards the specific task directions and/or demonstrates serious weaknesses in analytical writing.

A typical response in this category exhibits ONE OR MORE of the following characteristics:

a) is unclear or seriously limited in addressing the specific task directions and/or in presenting or developing a position on the issue

b) provides few, if any, relevant reasons or examples in support of its claims

c) is unfocused and/or disorganized

d) has serious problems in language and sentence structure that frequently interfere with meaning

e) contains serious errors in grammar, usage or mechanics that frequently obscure meaning

Score 1

A one response demonstrates fundamental deficiencies in analytical writing.

A typical response in this category exhibits ONE OR MORE of the following characteristics:

a) provides little or no evidence of understanding the issue

b) provides little evidence of the ability to develop an organized response (i.e., is extremely disorganized and/or extremely brief)

c) has severe problems in language and sentence structure that persistently interfere with meaning

d) contains pervasive errors in grammar, usage or mechanics that result in incoherence

Score 0

A typical response in this category is off topic (i.e., provides no evidence of an attempt to respond to the assigned topic), is in a foreign language, merely copies the topic, consists of only keystroke characters or is illegible or nonverbal.

Chapter **5**

Solved Argument Tasks with Strategies

General Strategies

The brief passages and directions in the Analyze an Argument task contain some complexity. In order to achieve a high score, you must understand the terminology. The following list is intended to help you clarify your written evaluation of the argument.

Although you do not need to know special analytical techniques and terminology, you should be familiar with the directions for the Argument task and with certain key concepts, including the following:

a) Is there an alternative explanation for the events in question that can invalidate, either in whole or in part, the explanation given in the passage?

b) How can I break the argument into its component parts to understand how they create the whole argument?

c) Can I identify the line of reasoning used to create the argument?

d) What does the author of the argument assume to be true for the argument to be true?

e) Does the line of reasoning validate the conclusion?

f) Can I imagine an example that refutes any or several of the statements in the argument?

g) Am I able to evaluate the argument based on the quality of the facts and reasons presented in it?

Regardless of the approach you take, you must present a well-developed evaluation of the argument. You should take brief notes when you identify the arguments claims, assumptions, and conclusion. Jot down as many alternative explanations as you can along with additional evidence that might support or refute the claims in the argument. Finally, list the changes in the argument that would make the reasoning more solid. It is more important to be specific than it is to have a long list of evidence and examples.

Use as many or as few paragraphs as you consider appropriate for your argument, but you should create a new paragraph when you move on to a new idea or example of support for your position. The GRE readers are not looking for a specific number of ideas or paragraphs. Instead, they are reading to determine the level of understanding of the topic and the complexity with which you respond.

You are free to organize and develop your response in any way you think will enable you to effectively communicate your evaluation of the argument. You may recall writing strategies that you learned in high school or a writing-intensive course that you took in college, but it is not necessary to employ any of those strategies. It is important that your ideas follow a logical progression and display strong critical thinking

Argument Task 1

Woven baskets characterized by a particular distinctive design pattern have previously been found only in the immediate vicinity of the prehistoric village of Palea and therefore were believed to have been made only by the Palean people. Recently, however, archaeologists discovered such a "Palean" basket in Lithos, an ancient village across the Brim River from Palea. The Brim River is very deep and broad, and so the ancient Paleans could have crossed it only by boat, and no Palean boats have been found. Thus it follows that the so-called Palean baskets were not uniquely Palean.

Write a response in which you discuss one or more alternative explanations that could rival the proposed explanation and explain how your explanation or explanations can plausibly account for the facts presented in the argument.

Strategies

Regardless of the approach you take, you must present a well-developed evaluation of the argument. You should take brief notes when you identify the arguments claims, assumptions, and conclusion. Jot down as many alternative explanations as you can along with additional evidence that might support or refute the claims in the argument. Finally, list the changes in the argument that would make the reasoning more solid. It is more important to be specific than it is to have a long list of evidence and examples.

This argument cites recent archaeological discoveries and geological features to support the claim that these baskets were made not only by the Palean people.

In developing your response you are asked to develop alternative explanations that could rival the explanation in the argument and explain how your explanation can account for the facts presented in the original explanation.

What conclusions and assumptions are either explicit or implied in the original explanation?

Facts and Assumptions:

a) The Brim River is very deep and broad.

   The implication is that this has always been the case. The river may have changed course or become larger over time.

b) The river could only have been crossed in boats.

   There can be several ways to cross a wide, deep river.

c) The Paleans had no boats.

   This assumption is based on the fact that no evidence of the Paleans' having boats exists. That is not to say that at some point in the future evidence of boats will not be found.

d) The Paleans could not have crossed the river.

   This assumption underlies the claim that may need qualifying.

e)   "Palean" baskets have been discovered in Lithos.

This fact underlies the claim that the baskets are not unique to Palea. The river itself could have carried baskets from one side of the river to the other.

f)   The baskets are Palean in origin.

This assumption is supported by the discovery of the baskets in Palea prior to their being discovered in Lithos.

Alternative Explanations:

a)   Geography is always changing. The Brim River may have followed a different course or been shallower or narrower at some point in time. Climate changes throughout the year may affect the depth and width of the river. Does the river become shallower and narrower as the spring runoff recedes?

b)   The Paleans may have been terrific swimmers. Depending on other geographical features, the Paleans may have worked with the residents of Lithos to construct a bridge across the river.

c)   The materials that the Paleans used to construct their boats may have disintegrated over time, leaving no evidence of their having existed. As archaeologists continue their work, they may uncover evidence of boats.

d)   It is difficult to imagine that any group of people would have let a geographical feature, like a river, remain an obstacle. If there were resources that the Paleans needed or wanted on the other side of the river, they would have found a way to cross it. This is assuming that the river either existed at all or existed in its current state.

e)   Because the baskets have been discovered on both sides of the river does not mean that they were carried there by people. It is possible that, during some flood, the baskets were lifted by the water itself and carried from one bank to the other.

f)   Because the baskets were discovered first in Palea, archaeologists assumed that they originated there. After their discovery in Lithos, it might be as correct to assume that the baskets originated there.

Your notes do not have to be exhaustive. As you begin to write your essay, your brain will generate new ideas. Make certain that you keep the directions in mind as you develop your ideas. Use as many or as few paragraphs as you consider appropriate for your argument, but you should create a new paragraph when you move on to a new idea or example of support for your position. The GRE readers are not looking for a specific number of ideas or paragraphs. Instead, they are reading to determine the level of understanding of the topic and the complexity with which you respond.

You are free to organize and develop your response in any way you think will enable you to effectively communicate your evaluation of the argument. You may recall writing strategies that you learned in high school or a writing-intensive course that you took in college, but it is not necessary to employ any of those strategies. It is important that your ideas follow a logical progression and display strong critical thinking.

Sample Essay

Rivers are not static geographical features. Spring rains and snow melt swell rivers to their maximum width and depth. As warmer, drier months arrive, the thirsty land absorbs water from the river, and evaporation takes its toll. If we consider the mighty Mississippi River that makes its way from its headwaters in Minnesota in the north to its terminus in the Gulf of Mexico in the south, we know that spring floods are inevitable along its entire course. At those times, the width of the river and the speed of its currents make it difficult to cross even with a boat. After summer arrives, the Mississippi becomes narrower and slower, and both barges and pleasure craft ply its waters with ease. The explanation presented here fails to state if the Brim River is very deep and wide throughout the year. It is just as likely that the river behaves much like the Mississippi and that travel across it is possible by means other than boats during the warmer, drier months of the year. The Paleans would have taken advantage of those conditions and used their unique baskets to carry goods to trade with the people of Lithos on the opposite bank.

To date no evidence exists to show that the Paleans had boats. For millennia, there was no evidence that Noah had built an ark, either, until what appeared to be the outline of a large vessel was found on the side of Mt. Ararat. Archaeological digs are ongoing events. Just as the baskets were found on the Lithosian side of the Brim River in recent times, it may be that evidence of Palean boats will be discovered as the study of the site continues. The boats were probably constructed of materials that would have disintegrated fairly rapidly if they existed at all. The assumption that they had none is based on missing evidence. Even assuming that the Brim River has always been wide and deep, means other than boats could have been used to cross it. Maybe the Paleans were terrific swimmers. Maybe they built rafts. Maybe they clung to logs and were carried across by the current. It is virtually impossible to prove or disprove any of these theories.

The fact that the baskets were found both in Palea and Lithos is open to a number of interpretations. Flooding of the river itself may be responsible for the migration of the baskets from one side to the other. The baskets may have been used at the river's edge to collect edible plants or fish, and some baskets may have been forgotten there. As the waters rose, the baskets were lifted and carried to the other bank. A shift in the course of the river may have divided what was once one village, leaving what became known as Palea on one side, Lithos on the other, and the distinctive baskets on both sides.

Archaeologists will likely continue to study this site. Until evidence is found to the contrary, their present conclusions may stand. That those conclusions are based on lack of evidence is not sufficient to abandon the search for artifacts that may alter them.

Argument Task 2

> *Twenty years ago, Dr. Field, a noted anthropologist, visited the island of Tertia. Using an observation-centered approach to studying Tertian culture, he concluded from his observations that children in Tertia were reared by an entire village rather than by their own biological parents. Recently another anthropologist, Dr. Karp, visited the group of islands that includes Tertia and used the interview-centered method to study child-rearing practices. In the interviews that Dr. Karp conducted with children living in this group of islands, the children spent much more time talking about their biological parents than about other adults in the village. Dr. Karp decided that Dr. Field's conclusion about Tertian village culture must be invalid. Some anthropologists recommend that to obtain accurate information on Tertian child-rearing practices, future research on the subject should be conducted via the interview-centered method.*
>
> Write a response in which you discuss what questions would need to be answered in order to decide whether the recommendation and the argument on which it is based are reasonable. Be sure to explain how the answers to these questions would help to evaluate the recommendation.

Strategies

Regardless of the approach you take, consider the following steps:

a) Is there an alternative explanation for the events in question that can invalidate, either in whole or in part, the explanation given in the passage?

b) How can I break the argument into its component parts to understand how they create the whole argument?

c) Can I identify the line of reasoning used to create the argument?

d) What does the author of the argument assume to be true for the argument to be true?

e) Does the line of reasoning validate the conclusion?

f) Can I imagine an example that refutes any or several of the statements in the argument?

g) Am I able to evaluate the argument based on the quality of the facts and reasons presented in it?

Based on your responses to all or some of these questions, you must present a well-developed evaluation of the argument. You should take brief notes when you identify the arguments claims, assumptions, and conclusion. Jot down as many alternative explanations as you can along with additional evidence that might support or refute the claims in the argument. Finally, list the changes in the argument that would make the reasoning more solid. It is more important to be specific than it is to have a long list of evidence and examples.

This argument cites the results of two studies concerning child-rearing practices on the island of Tertia and the group of islands that includes Tertia and makes a recommendation about further research.

In developing your response, you are required to generate questions that will help you decide if the recommendation and the argument on which it is based are reasonable and then explain how the answers to your questions would help evaluate the recommendation. It might be helpful to isolate the recommendation.

Recommendation:

To obtain accurate information on Tertian child-rearing practices, future research on the subject should be conducted via the interview-centered method.

Next, identify the argument's conclusions and the evidence that led to those conclusions.

Claims and assumptions:

a)   Dr. Field's conclusion about Tertian village culture must be invalid. This assumption supports the recommendation to conduct further studies using the interview-based approach. Later studies seem to negate Field's findings.

b)   The observation – centered approach yields inaccurate results. This unstated assumption underlies the recommendation that, in order to obtain accurate results, further studies should be conducted using the interview-based approach.

c)   The interview-centered method yields accurate results. The conclusions in Karp's research seem to justify this conclusion. This assumption supports the recommendation.

d)   Some anthropologists recommend the interview-centered approach for future research.

e)   You should now be able to generate some questions that could clarify or weaken the argument.

Questions:

a)   If the interview-centered approach had been used before the observation-centered approach, would the second results have invalidated those first results?

b)   What kinds of questions were included in the interviews?

c)   What outside influences may have arisen in the twenty years between the two studies? Have the women in the islands gone outside of the home to work? Have television and/or the Internet become available? Think about the ways in which your own community has changed in the last twenty years.

d)   Has the family structure undergone any changes in the twenty years between the two studies? Are families having fewer children?

e)   What other islands were included in Dr. Karp's study? Were child-rearing practices similar on all of the islands?

f)   Are the results of each study both valid and reliable? Did the studies indeed measure what they were intended to measure? If the same study were done again, would the results be the same?

g)   Did Dr. Fields' study make the people of Tertia reconsider their method of child-rearing? His questions may have caused them to reflect upon the way they perform this task.

Your notes do not have to be exhaustive. As you begin to write your essay, your brain will generate new ideas. Make certain that you keep the directions in mind as you develop your ideas. Use as many or as few paragraphs as you consider appropriate for your argument, but you should create a new paragraph when you move on to a new idea or example of support for your position. The GRE readers are not looking for a specific number of ideas or paragraphs. Instead, they are reading to determine the level of understanding of the topic and the complexity with which you respond.

You are free to organize and develop your response in any way you think will enable you to effectively communicate your evaluation of the argument. You may recall writing strategies that you learned in high school or a writing-intensive course that you took in college, but it is not necessary to employ any of those strategies. It is important that your ideas follow a logical progression and display strong critical thinking.

Sample Essay

Change in virtually every society around the world is occurring at almost lightning speed. Tertia and the group of islands to which it belongs are not likely to be immune to change. If we assume that Dr. Field's conclusions were appropriate twenty years ago, we must ask ourselves if events during the intervening years may have changed the child-rearing practices that he observed. Exposure to other people visiting the island, access to television and the Internet, and even people leaving the island would influence future studies of the culture. Dr. Field's study, alone, could have caused the residents of Tertia to question their child-rearing practices and, as a result, modify them. Dr. Karp's recent study, regardless of the technique he used, could not fail to yield different results than the earlier study. Playing devil's advocate for a moment, let's reverse the order of the studies. Assume that Dr. Karp completed his study using the interview-centered approach and that, twenty years later Dr. Field arrived at the island and used his observation-centered approach to complete his study. The results would most certainly still disagree with each other. In this case, do Dr. Field's results invalidate those of Dr. Karp?

The scope of each study appears to be different, as well. Dr. Field allegedly studied only the families on the island of Tertia while Dr. Karp visited the group of islands that includes Tertia. The fact that the subjects were different for each event is enough to nullify one's superiority over the other. It also appears that Dr. Field observed the culture of Tertia as a whole, while Karp focused on child-rearing practices. Having used two variants of research procedures, the anthropologists were destined to achieve unreliable results.

We should take a closer look at the approaches that each anthropologist adopted. As Field employed the observation-centered method to study the culture of Tertia, what did he observe in addition to child-rearing practices? One could infer that those practices were a small, perhaps even minor, portion of his entire project. On the other hand, Karp's project, using an interview-centered method, seems to have ignored other aspects of the culture. Why would a group of scientists use these disparate studies as a basis for further research?

Overall, the results of these studies have too much dissimilarity and leave too many questions unanswered to use them as justification for more research using either one of the methods mentioned in the argument. The author of the argument may have more information than he has seen fit to reveal and, thus, may be qualified to sit in judgment of the methods and the results. However, based on what has been revealed here, the recommendation is based on flawed reasoning.

Argument Task 3

> In surveys Mason City residents rank water sports (swimming, boating, and fishing) among their favorite recreational activities. The Mason River flowing through the city is rarely used for these pursuits, however, and the city park department devotes little of its budget to maintaining riverside recreational facilities. For years there have been complaints from residents about the quality of the river's water and the river's smell. In response, the state has recently announced plans to clean up Mason River. Use of the river for water sports is, therefore, sure to increase. The city government should for that reason devote more money in this year's budget to riverside recreational facilities.
>
> Write a response in which you examine the stated and/or unstated assumptions of the argument. Be sure to explain how the argument depends on these assumptions and what the implications are for the argument if the assumptions prove unwarranted on.

Strategies

The first step in performing your analysis consists of identifying the texts' key point, recommendation, prediction or hypothesis. All the other arguments and assumptions are designed to support this central claim. In this case, the author attempts to argue that "The city government should devote more money to riverside recreational facilities".

The next step would involve creating a statement that summarizes the text by including the central claim and its supporting arguments.

Given the Mason City surveys ranking water sports as the favorite recreation activity of the residents and the upcoming river cleansing project that is thought to eliminate the cause for the low river usage, the author of the text argues for an increase in this year's budget devoted to riverside recreational facilities.

The easiest way to break down an argument into implicit assumptions is to look at the ideas that support each core (explicit) assumption. Ideally, it would be good to have at least three implicit assumptions for every explicit one. However, keep in mind that you likely won't have time enough to expound on all of them in your essay. When writing your argument it's good to lay down the ideas like in the format below – it will help you easily determine which explicit assumptions are undermined/strengthened by the implicit argument you are analyzing.

Assumptions

Explicit Assumptions	Implicit Assumptions
Survey accurately reflects people's opinions on water sports	• There are no biased or leading questions • The survey demographics are representative of the city (city and survey demographics are similar) • The studies have a low standard deviation (enough people participated, so that a small group's opinion cannot skew the results) • People that rank water sports as high will also participate in them
River pollution is responsible for the low usage of the city river	• The complaints are representative for the city • River pollution is the only reason why people do not use the river
Cleaning up the river will increase usage for water sports	• There are no other outlets for water sports in the city • The smell of the river is due to pollution and not a naturally occurring event (sulphur) • The quality of the water is due to pollution and not a natural occurring event (mineral deposits) • Residents would like to use the river for water sports • The clean-up will end pollution/is extensive
The increase in usage is sufficient to justify increasing the budget for riverside recreational facilities	• A great percentage of people will go to the riverside • The people that go to the riverside need facilities • Riverside facilities are dedicated to water sports (and not other pursuits) • Current riverside facilities are insufficient • The clean-up of the river will happen in a short term (enough to justify making changes to this year's budget)

After having established your assumptions you need to take care of the second part of your essay, namely the implications for the main claim should the assumptions be unwarranted. A good way to go about writing this part is to think of examples of situations that may contradict each implicit assumption. The examples are not vital; you can still build a case by directly stating "if assumption 'A' proves to be untrue, the". However, including the contradicting situations will help enrich your essay and ultimately get you a higher score.

The next step would be to create a 'logic tree' to see how disproving an assumption will affect the other arguments down the line. The branch of the logic tree will follow this line: implicit assumption affects explicit assumptions which in turn relate to the main argument.

For instance, in our case:

Implicit Assumption	Contradicting Situations	Effect on Explicit Assumption	Effect on Main Argument
River pollution is the only reason why people do not use the river	• River is too distant • Very fast currents	• Somewhat weaken or disprove the assumption (people might still not use the river after it is cleaned)	• Building more facilities would become useless, if river usage will not increase • Waste of resources
The smell of the river is due to pollution and not a naturally occurring event	• Sulfur • Natural gas leaks (Cattaraugus Creek)	• Cleaning the river will not remove the odor • Cleaning the river will not increase river usage	• Building more facilities would become useless, if river usage will not increase • Waste of resources
The complaints are representative for the city	• Low percentage of people complaining • An individual filing a large number of complaints	• The complaints do not reflect the resident's opinions about the river • River usage might not increase by solving the complaints	• Building more facilities would become useless, if river usage will not increase • Main cause of low river usage remains unknown

Sample Essay

Given the Mason City surveys ranking water sports as the favorite recreation activity of the residents and the upcoming river cleansing project that is thought to eliminate the cause for the low river usage, the author of the text argues for an increase in this year's budget devoted to riverside recreational facilities. The author of the proposal makes suggestions that can prove to be very costly especially if the assumptions on which the case rests prove to be unwarranted.

When arguing for the increased revenue allocated to this year's budget for riverside facilities, the author draws upon data from surveys conducted in Mason City. One of the main assumptions that the case rests on is that the surveys that were conducted accurately reflect people's opinions on water sports. In taking this data at face value, the author further assumes that the survey demographics are representative for the entirety of the city. The most essential part of any research is the methodology – in this case, if the survey takers asked only people that live next to the river or only citizens of a certain age, then that can very well mean that the rest of the citizens do not view water sports as a favorite activity, in which case, regardless of the river cleaning actions, the actual usage of the waterway will not increase.

Another implicit assumption related to the idea that the surveys accurately reflect people's opinions on water sports is the notion that the research methodology is sound, namely there are no biased or leading questions. Phrasing survey questions is sometimes likened to an art – just like any activity that requires a considerable amount of skill and knowledge. Should the surveys contain badly phrased questions, like an option to choose between water sports or extreme activities, then the results of the surveys would no longer be reliable. In this example, most people would choose water sports because it is the less extreme/unreasonable option and not because they would like to actively engage in this type of sporting activity. In this case, a budgetary increase for riverside facilities could prove to be a waste of money, since people's interests lie elsewhere, and not with river based activities. The same conclusion would apply if the questions were biased due to the personal interest of the survey researchers (a company providing water sports equipment can be unwittingly biased and skewer the results in favor of water sports activities simply by placing the focus of the questionnaire on said type of activity).

Another line of reasoning that the author uses to support his argument is the idea that river pollution and odor are responsible for the low usage of the city river. This argument is based on several other assumptions like the notion that the complaints received about river odor and pollution are representative for the city and the idea that there are no other possible explanations as to why the river usage is low. It is entirely within the realm of possibility that the overall number of complaints, when reported to the total number of citizens, is very low. Or, if the number of complaints is high, it may well be that only a small number of people are responsible for them (in the sense that a single person files a large number of complaints). In both of these instances, the complaints prove not to be representative for the overall opinion of the citizens. If that is the case, and this assumption is unwarranted, then the upcoming cleaning of the river will not address the main cause of the low river usage and the number of people engaging in sporting activities on the waterway will remain unaffected. As such, increasing the budget for riverside facilities would be pointless, not to mention costly.

The other assumption supporting the idea that the river pollution and odor are responsible for the low usage of the city river is the notion that there are no other possible explanations as to why the river usage is low. If there are other reasons why people don't like to use the Mason City river, like the distance to the river or the presence of strong currents, then the cleaning of the river would fail to address the people's main concerns with the waterway, and river usage will not increase.

These lines of inquiry lead directly to another main assumption on which the author rests his case for increasing the amount of money allocated to riverside facilities. The author assumes that cleaning up the river will increase the river's usage for water sports. When advocating for this line of thought, the author assumes that the smell and quality of the water are due to pollution, and not naturally occurring events. Sulfur in the water can give it a rotten egg smell, or the presence of natural gas in the river banks can create a foul odor. As for the water quality, mineral deposits in the water or an abundance of underwater plant life can give the river an unappealing look. These are just some of the possible alternate explanation for the river's odor and water quality. If there are natural causes for the look and odor of the river, then cleaning the river will not get rid of either problem. Provided that most citizens consider the river's look and odor to be the main deterrent against doing sporting activities on the Mason City river, then river usage would not increase with the cleansing of the river. As such, the proposal to increase funds for riverside facilities would not be supported by a rise in actual usage of those facilities.

When proposing to increase the money allocated to the riverside facilities in Mason City, the author of the argument assumes that there will be a sufficient increase in river usage to justify taking these budgetary measures. An implicit assumption of this argument is the idea that a great percentage of people will go to the riverside. If, for instance, there are a lot of water sport outlets in town, due to the river being unappealing and the resident of Mason City loving water-based activities, then it's entirely likely that even after the river is made accessible, a great percentage of the population will continue to use those outlets (especially since they like to offer subscriptions). Should that be the case, and the number of people that would go to the riverside would be low, then there would be no justification to increase the budget for riverside facilities.

All in all, when making the case for increasing the budget for the riverside facilities in Mason City, the author of the proposal makes a series of assumptions that are not backed by evidence and would require further investigation. Spending taxpayer money always needs good justification – without a more thorough investigation, the author risks of drawing inaccurate conclusions which will lead to making ineffective or costly suggestions.

Argument Task 4

Two years ago, radio station WCQP in Rockville decided to increase the number of call-in advice programs that it broadcast; since that time, its share of the radio audience in the Rockville listening area has increased significantly. Given WCQP's recent success with call-in advice programming, and citing a nationwide survey indicating that many radio listeners are quite interested in such programs, the station manager of KICK in Medway recommends that KICK include more call-in advice programs in an attempt to gain a larger audience share in its listening area.

Write a response in which you discuss what questions would need to be answered in order to decide whether the recommendation is likely to have the predicted result. Be sure to explain how the answers to these questions would help to evaluate the recommendation.

Strategies

The first step in performing your analysis consists of identifying the texts' key point, recommendation, prediction or hypothesis. All the other arguments and assumptions are designed to support this central claim. In this case, the author attempts to demonstrate that "more call-in advice program will increase the stations' listener ratings".

The next step would involve creating a statement that summarizes the text by including the central claim and its supporting arguments.

The station manager of KICK recommends increasing the number of call-in advice programs that are being broadcasted in order to gain a larger audience, given that a similar strategy has worked for a radio station in another town, and a national survey indicates that people are interested in such programs.

When considering what questions are needed to evaluate the arguments outlined in the text, it is important to keep in mind that arguments are based on assumptions – points that are taken to be true, without need for proof. This is what you need to look for – explicit and implicit assumptions, since they lack the evidence required to prove their validity.

Assumptions

Explicit Assumptions	Implicit Assumptions
WCQP's increase in listeners is due to the additional call-in advice programs	• There were no other internal factors that could have contributed to WCQP's increase in listener ratings • There were no other external (economical) factors that could have contributed to the increase in listener ratings • The increase in listener ratings is for the call-in advice time slot • The increase in listeners was significant
The national survey accurately reflects the preferences of Medway's population	• Demographics of both Medway and the survey are compatible • The survey findings are conclusive
The strategy applied in Rockville is applicable in Medway	• Rockville and Medway have similar target audience demographics • WCQP and KICK have similar market situations • WCQP and KICK are comparable in terms of size and popularity
KICK's audience will increase with more call-in advice programs	• Medway's radio listener market size is big enough to support the potential audience growth • There is a need for call-in advice programs • The need for call-in advice programs was not met elsewhere

Sample Essay

The station manager of KICK recommends increasing the number of call-in advice programs that are being broadcasted in order to gain a larger audience, given that a similar strategy has worked for a radio station in another town, and a national survey indicates that people are interested in such programs. Like all changes to a business' approach, the recommendation made by KICK's manager carries with it a risk of failure, and as such needs to be thoroughly analyzed before any decisions of implementing the suggested strategy are made.

In outlining his reasoning for the recommendation, the station manager of KICK rests his case on the assumption that WCQP's increase in listeners is due to the additional call-in advice programs. The first question that comes into mind, in this case, is if there were any other internal and external factors that could have contributed to the increase in listeners, such as a shutdown of one of WCQP's major competitors, the start of a WCQP promotional campaign or the station acquiring a popular radio host. Having a great number of other plausible explanations for WCQP's success would significantly weaken the premise that more call-in advice programs would have the desired effect on KICK's listener basis. However, should the answer to the question prove that the increase in call-in advice programs is the sole or major reason responsible for the listener audience boost then it becomes plausible that WCQP's success can be replicated by KICK, given additional compatibility points like market analysis data.

The next inquiry point related to WCQP's success would investigate during which time slot the WCQP listener ratings increased and how significant was this increase. This data can serve to research whether the listener increase is statistically relevant. A rise in listener ratings of 1%, while technically still considered an increase, would mean that adding more call-in advice programs is a costly method with no substantial benefits and the station managers should consider alternate means of bolstering listener ratings. From the other perspective, should it turn out that the increase in audience market shares is a dramatic one, then KICK's managers should give the WCQP's strategy due consideration.

When making his case for increasing the amount of call-in advice programs the station manager cites the results of a national survey as compelling evidence that there is a great desire for programs of this type. When handling surveys and statistic data it is always important to look not only at the results but also at the theoretical framework and methodology of the study being conducted, in order to be able to ascertain whether the reasoning is sound, or if the scientists have missed some crucial aspect or mitigating factor. As such, the station manager should inquire as to how accurate are the study findings. Should the methodology be faulty, like having a small sample size with a big standard deviation, or constructing the survey questions in a leading manner, then the results would no longer be indicative of the people's desire for listening to call-in programs, and the station manager would have to find alternative means of estimating the potential market size, lest his argument becomes significantly weakened. A properly conducted survey can serve to strengthen the station manager's recommendation – most market analyses are based on such type of direct information gathering.

If the survey findings are accurate, then the next step would be to determine whether these results are applicable to the population of Medway. The station manager should ask himself if the survey and Medway's demographics are compatible. If this assumption holds true, then the manager has accurately pinpointed a current need of the Medway population and the recommendation to satisfy said need by changing their programs would be more warranted. But national studies deal with averages; therefore it is possible that what might be true for the general population is not necessarily true for a particular subgroup. For instance, a national study that identified the preferred musical genres as rock and oldies might not be so applicable to specific cases, like towns from the bible belt. Should the demographics not be comparable, then the national survey that is at the center of the station manager's argument would not accurately reflect the preferences of the local population of Medway. In order to strengthen his argument, the station manager would have to look at radio preference indicators that are specific to Medway.

The station manager's assumption that the strategy applied in Rockville is applicable in Medway begets the question of how similar the Medway and Rockville markets and target audiences are to each other. If the target audience demographics and the market conditions like the number of competitors, market size or degree of popularity are relatively similar, then implementing the suggested strategy would be a very good course of action, given the high likelihood of replicating WCQP's success. Not only that, but the similarity can make the strategy very cost effective and provide KICK with a readymade implementation roadmap that has a high probability of increasing the company's profits. However, if the market and target audiences of the two cities are different, then the assumption that the strategy applied in Rockville is applicable in Medway is significantly weakened, because there is a high likelihood that WCQP's success strategy might not be suitable for the population of Medway. In order to deal with this possibility, the station manager would have to adapt the finer points of WCQP's strategy to the needs of the Medway population, in which case his recommendation might still be valid. Current trendsetting strategies also rely heavily on the reuse of successful strategies with adaptations made to suit each company's specific situation.

All in all, before arguing for the implementation of a strategy used by a different radio station, KICK's station manager should consider whether the market conditions in the two towns are similar enough to warrant making the suggested change. The manager should also consider how to adapt the strategies if the markets prove to be too different, or completely reorient himself to other strategies, based on market demands.

Argument Task 5

> *The following is a recommendation from the personnel director to the president of Acme Publishing Company.*
>
> *"Many other companies have recently stated that having their employees take the Easy Read Speed-Reading Course has greatly improved productivity. One graduate of the course was able to read a 500-page report in only two hours; another graduate rose from an assistant manager to vice president of the company in under a year. Obviously, the faster you can read, the more information you can absorb in a single workday. Moreover, Easy Read would cost Acme only $500 per employee - a small price to pay when you consider the benefits. Included in this fee is a three-week seminar in Spruce City and a lifelong subscription to the Easy Read newsletter. Clearly, Acme would benefit greatly by requiring all of our employees to take the Easy Read course."*
>
> Write a response in which you discuss what specific evidence is needed to evaluate the argument and explain how the evidence would weaken or strengthen the argument.

Strategies

A good place to start your analysis is by creating a statement that reveals the main idea of the argument. Although the writer is creating an argument, he may ultimately be stating a position, making a recommendation, or making a prediction. It may be helpful for you to determine which of these formats is most evident in the argument.

Based on examples from other companies, the personnel director at Acme Publishing Company is recommending the Easy Read Speed-Reading course as a means of benefiting Acme Publishing Company.

Assumptions:

a) Easy Read Speed-Reading Course increases productivity in the workplace.

b) Graduates of the course are more likely to be promoted.

c) People who read faster absorb more information.

d) Benefits of taking the course outweigh the cost.

e) Productivity needs to be improved at Acme Publishing Company.

Evidence needed:

a) The ability for employees to read faster is important to productivity at Acme Publishing Company.

b) The percentage of employees whose jobs require them to read rapidly.

c) The manner in which employees are promoted at Acme Publishing Company.

d) The focus of businesses that have seen greater productivity after their workers completed the speed-reading course.

e) The cost of travel for employees of Acme Publishing Company to travel and stay in Spruce City.

f) The effect on Acme Publishing Company of its employees' being gone for three weeks.

g) Other factors in addition to speed reading that led to the employee's promotion

h) Reading faster leads to greater knowledge.

i) The productivity of Acme workers.

After completing these steps, you should have enough material to write your analysis. Remember that you are not creating a position of your own; you are evaluating the strengths and weaknesses of the existing argument. You do not have to include all of the points that you have created in your prewriting. In fact, during the process of drafting your analysis, other ideas may come to mind, and, if they strengthen your analysis, you should include them.

Sample Essay

Companies are always looking for ways to improve the efficiency of their workers. Time is money, and the more that employees can accomplish in a workday, the more money the company is likely to make. Methods to increase productivity must be tailored to the type of work being done and the results desired by the company. Acme Publishing Company's owners need evidence of the benefit to be derived from the speed reading course before investing both time and money.

The ability to speed read is important in some occupations. Students doing research can benefit from quickly reading through documents in order to extract pertinent facts. Lawyers frequently wade through volumes of documents or case law, and the ability to speed read can save them a lot of time. Acme Publishing Company should determine how many of its employees actually need to read more quickly in order to perform more efficiently. The focus of the business may not include voluminous reading, so spending the money on the course for all of Acme's employees would not be a wise use of resources. Committing to a three-week retreat for all employees may be unrealistic. If the retreat is scheduled for only one three-week period, Acme Publishing Company would have to shut down to send all of its workers, potentially leading to a loss of business. The company may decide that some of its workers could become more productive after taking the speed-reading course and attending the retreat which would cost much less while, perhaps, making those employees feel more positive about their jobs.

The personnel manager cites examples of employees at one or more other companies who increased their reading speed or got promotions after taking the course. It would be helpful to know how rapidly the first employee read 500 pages before taking the course and whether or not reading faster was the main objective of his job. Evidence should also be forthcoming that the assistant manager's receiving a promotion was a direct result of taking the speed-reading course. That employee may have been in line to become vice president anyway based on his or her other qualifications. The president of Acme Publishing Company also needs evidence that the two employees cited work for a company whose goals and objectives are similar to those of Acme. If the other company involves vastly different work or product than Acme Publishing, then the examples are irrelevant. The ability to read rapidly may not be a factor in earning promotions at Acme Publishing. Evaluating the strength of this argument would be easier if the reader knows the criteria that Acme uses when selecting candidates for higher positions in the company.

Before accepting this recommendation, the company president should ask for evidence about his workers' level of productivity at all tasks required by Acme. The evidence may show that all of his workers meet established productivity levels, making the speed-reading course unnecessary. He may find that productivity levels are subpar in areas where the ability to read quickly is not a factor. On the other hand, he may find lower productivity in departments where a course in speed-reading would help those workers perform better. This evidence can help the president determine which of his personnel can help the Company move forward by completing the recommended course.

The president of Acme Publishing needs evidence that speed reading leads to the absorption of more knowledge. Because more knowledge is important in virtually every industry, this evidence could prove the value of the course to the company and its employees. Lack of this evidence negates the personnel director's conclusion that the money spent on the speed reading course would be a wise use of company resources.

Argument Task 6

The following appeared in a memorandum from the owner of Movies Galore, a chain of movie-rental stores.

"In order to reverse the recent decline in our profits, we must reduce operating expenses at Movies Galore's ten movie-rental stores. Since we are famous for our special bargains, raising our rental prices is not a viable way to improve profits. Last month our store in downtown Marston significantly decreased its operating expenses by closing at 6:00 p.m. rather than 9:00 p.m. and by reducing its stock by eliminating all movies released more than five years ago. Therefore, in order to increase profits without jeopardizing our reputation for offering great movies at low prices, we recommend implementing similar changes in our other nine Movies Galore stores."

Write a response in which you discuss what questions would need to be answered in order to decide whether the recommendation and the argument on which it is based are reasonable. Be sure to explain how the answers to these questions would help to evaluate the recommendation.

Strategies

A good place to start your analysis is by creating a statement that reveals the main idea of the argument. Although the writer is creating an argument, he may ultimately be stating a position, making a recommendation, or making a prediction. It may be helpful for you to determine which of these formats is most evident in the argument.

The owner of Movies Galore is recommending the same changes in all of his stores that he made in his downtown Marston location as a means of reversing a decline in profits.

Assumptions:

 a) Reducing expenses is the best way for Movies Galore to increase profits.

 b) The changes made at the downtown Marston location will be successful at the other stores.

 c) Low prices are the major reason people patronize Movies Galore.

 d) Movies older than five years attract fewer customers than other genres or newer releases.

 e) The downtown Marston location is busiest between opening and 6:00 pm.

 f) The downtown Marston location is not busy enough between 6:00 and 9:00 pm to justify staying open during those hours.

Questions:

 a) Have profits declined at all or just some of the stores?

 b) Have profits increased at the downtown Marston store?

c)   During which hours is each store busiest?

d)   Has the owner tried other means of reducing expenses?

e)   Why do customers choose Movies Galore?

f)   Are older videos in high demand at any of the locations?

g)   Has the owner made some recent changes that have had a negative impact on profits?

After completing these steps, you should have enough material to write your analysis. Remember that you are not creating a position of your own; you are evaluating the strengths and weaknesses of the existing argument. You do not have to include all of the points that you have created in your prewriting. In fact, during the process of drafting your analysis, other ideas may come to mind, and, if they strengthen your analysis, you should include them.

Sample Essay

The owner of Movies Galore has made a sweeping recommendation with a view to increasing profits for his business. Before adopting the recommendation at all of his locations, he or she needs to answer some pointed questions. One size may not fit all. Each location should be analyzed individually by examining the answers to the questions.

First, he should ask if each store is experiencing a decline in profitability. He may find that only one or two of the stores are creating the decline in profits. Those which are making money for the company should likely be left alone. Even though all of them may be losing money, each may need an individual, specific adjustment to reverse the trend. This owner should also ask what the successful stores may be doing that the others are not. The answer may lead him to make changes different from the ones in the argument.

Shortening the hours of operation and eliminating some inventory will certainly reduce expenses, but the tactic doesn't always contribute to greater profits. Has the downtown Marston store generated higher profits since the changes were made? If that store was not habitually busy between the hours of 6:00 and 9:00, then the relatively minor loss of revenue may be offset by a fairly significant decrease in operating expenses. Electricity, heat, and wages for three hours can be substantial and are aspects of a business operation that can be controlled. Was there very little demand for older videos in that location as well? If so, then money spent on inventory can be better used to stock videos in greater demand by customers in this particular store.

Assuming that the owner has made the correct business decisions for the downtown location, it might be logical to apply the same changes to the other Movies Galore stores. Do all of the other locations experience a lack of business after 6:00? Any stores located in or near a mall may be busiest during the evening hours. Malls are generally open until 9:00 at night, and a store that closes at 6:00 will not be able to take advantage of traffic generated by the other shops.

The owner of Movies Galore assumes that the low prices account for the stores' popularity, but is that really the reason that customers choose them? Movies Galore may have the best selection of the videos most in demand. The stores' locations may be convenient and have plenty of free parking. They may have a great selection of movie snacks. The staff may be friendly and helpful. Without surveying his customers, the owner could be holding onto an idea that has little to support it.

Has the owner attempted any other changes to improve profits? He could increase revenues by expanding the selection of movie snacks and training his associates to suggest patrons buy them with every rental. Customers may have abandoned Movies Galore because the videos are not organized logically, or the associates deliver poor service. Has the owner made some recent changes that have led to a temporary decline in profits? Upgrading heating systems or lighting fixtures, for example, can be costly one-time expenditures that can account for the current lack of profitability. The owner may have new employees or managers that are undercharging for rentals or who may be stealing from the company.

Are other, similar businesses in the area experiencing a similar decline in profits? If so, Movies Galore's owner may have to look at his problem in an entirely different light. The market may be over saturated with movie rental businesses. People's rental habits may have changed in recent years by using video-on-demand features through their television cable companies or by subscribing to services like Netflix. When he examines the answers to all of the questions, the owner of Movies Galore will make better-informed decisions about his business.

Argument Task 7

> *Evidence suggests that academic honor codes, which call for students to agree not to cheat in their academic endeavors and to notify a faculty member if they suspect that others have cheated, are far more successful than are other methods at deterring cheating among students at colleges and universities. Several years ago, Groveton College adopted such a code and discontinued its old-fashioned system in which teachers closely monitored students. Under the old system, teachers reported an average of thirty cases of cheating per year. In the first year the honor code was in place, students reported twenty-one cases of cheating; five years later, this figure had dropped to fourteen. Moreover, in a recent survey, a majority of Groveton students said that they would be less likely to cheat with an honor code in place than without.*
>
> Write a response in which you discuss one or more alternative explanations that could rival the proposed explanation and explain how your explanation(s) can plausibly account for the facts presented in the argument.

NOTE: *The above topic has wording similar to Argument Task 15 of GRE Analytical Writing Solutions to the Real Essay Topics Book 1. However, if you read carefully you will notice that the task instructions are different. Hence, it is very important to read the topic as well as its instructions completely before you start to write your response.*

Strategies

A good place to start your analysis is by creating a statement that reveals the main idea of the argument. Although the writer is creating an argument, he may ultimately be stating a position, making a recommendation, or making a prediction. It may be helpful for you to determine which of these formats is most evident in the argument.

The argument states the position that an honor code is a more effective means of curtailing cheating than close supervision by professors, and evidence at Groveton College appears to support the author's explanation.

Assumptions:

a)   Instances of cheating have declined since instituting an honor code.

b)   Between years one and five under the honor code system, instances of cheating continually declined.

c)   Enrollment at the college has remained the same during the five years of the honor code.

d)   Students are as likely to report cheating as are professors.

Alternative explanations:

a)   Students are less likely to report on their peers, thereby reducing the number of recorded cases of cheating.

b)   The college increased the severity of consequences for cheating when adopting the honor code.

c)   Students may not recognize some forms of cheating.

d)   Students don't have the opportunity to observe cheating.

e)   The school may have changed its grading system.

f)   Instructors may have adjusted their curriculum and assessments.

After completing these steps, you should have enough material to write your analysis. Remember that you are not creating a position of your own; you are evaluating the strengths and weaknesses of the existing argument. You do not have to include all of the points that you have created in your prewriting. In fact, during the process of drafting your analysis, other ideas may come to mind, and, if they strengthen your analysis, you should include them.

Sample Essay

The argument promotes the effectiveness of using an honor code to prevent cheating and uses some scant evidence to justify its continued use. An apparent decline in the number of cheating incidents leads the reader to agree with the position, but other explanations may be more realistic.

Students are not as likely to observe, recognize, or report cheating as are their professors. In a testing situation, for example, students may be so focused on their own performance and completing the test on time that they are unaware of others around them. Given the opportunity to look at other students in the classroom, they might not recognize that a fellow test- taker is cheating. Many who cheat have developed techniques that make their dishonest behavior invisible to the casual or inexperienced observer. Students who do see and recognize another's cheating are faced with a moral dilemma. On one hand, they have agreed to honor the code established by the college. On the other hand, they may risk losing a friend or causing the failure of an otherwise honest student. They may empathize with a classmate who chooses cheating as a means of passing a difficult course. Of course, cheating on a test is not the only form of academic dishonesty. Plagiarism rears its ugly head when students are under some pressure to meet a deadline for a research paper. The temptation to cut-and-paste and take credit for another's words or ideas is strong for college students who have run out of ideas before running out of time. Other students are not likely to see this type of work done by classmates and, therefore, cannot be expected to report it. The professors who do read and recognize the plagiarized writing are no longer compelled to report it. They may simply assign a grade of zero. These limitations can help to explain the lower number of reported incidents of cheating at Groveton College.

The adoption of the honor code by itself may not fully explain the apparent decline in cheating. School officials may have added new consequences or strengthened those that already existed if students are caught cheating in some manner. Fear of failure or expulsion would have created a greater incentive to remain academically honest at Groveton College.

In addition to instituting an honor code, Groveton College may have changed its grading system. They may have replaced a traditional 4-point measurement of excellence to pass/fail, for example. Relieved of the pressure to achieve based on rigid guidelines, students would feel less compelled to cheat in order to meet grading expectations. In addition, professors may have changed the nature of their assessments. Instead of administering tests in a pressurized classroom under time constraints, they may have given take-home tests that students can complete in the comfort of their own residences, using notes and other resources. They may have eliminated tests altogether, relying on measurements of knowledge that are less likely to create opportunities for cheating.

Perhaps the simplest explanation for a reduction in the number of reported instances of cheating would be a decline in student population at Groveton College. In fact, the college may have instituted the apparently popular honor code in an effort to attract more students to its campus. Depending on the size of the student body, a reduction in the number of reported cases of cheating could be an increase in the percentage of students caught cheating.

Groveton's use of the survey results in which a majority of students said they would be less likely to cheat if an honor code exists may be short-sighted. The survey may not have included other incentives to curtail cheating. If the survey listed only an honor code as a choice, the conclusion is flawed and is not likely to explain the apparent reduction in reported cheating cases.

If any of these alternate explanations sufficiently account for the lower number of reported cases of cheating at Groveton College, the school must relinquish its belief that the honor code is an effective change in its academic philosophy. Further investigation by college administrators can uncover the real reason for an increase in academic integrity.

Argument Task 8

> The following was written as a part of an application for a small-business loan by a group of developers in the city of Monroe.
>
> "A jazz music club in Monroe would be a tremendously profitable enterprise. Currently, the nearest jazz club is 65 miles away; thus, the proposed new jazz club in Monroe, the C-Note, would have the local market all to itself. Plus, jazz is extremely popular in Monroe: over 100,000 people attended Monroe's annual jazz festival last summer; several well-known jazz musicians live in Monroe; and the highest-rated radio program in Monroe is 'Jazz Nightly,' which airs every weeknight at 7 P.M. Finally, a nationwide study indicates that the typical jazz fan spends close to $1,000 per year on jazz entertainment."
>
> Write a response in which you discuss what specific evidence is needed to evaluate the argument and explain how the evidence would weaken or strengthen the argument.

NOTE: *The above topic has wording similar to Argument Task 28 of GRE Analytical Writing Solution to the Real Essay Topics - Book 2. However, if you read carefully you will notice that the task instructions are different. Hence, it is very important to read the topic as well as its instructions completely before you start to write your response.*

Strategies

The first step in performing your analysis consists of identifying the texts' key point, recommendation, prediction or hypothesis. All the other arguments and assumptions are designed to support this central claim. In this case, the author attempts to demonstrate that "A *jazz club in Monroe would be profitable*".

The next step would involve creating a statement that summarizes the text by including the central claim and its supporting arguments.

The authors of the loan application argue that a jazz club in Monroe would be profitable because the town boasts a big jazz fan base and the nearest competitor is located very far away.

When considering the evidence that is necessary to support the arguments outlined in the text, it is important to keep in mind that arguments are based on assumptions – points that are taken to be true, without need for proof. This is what you need to look for – explicit and implicit assumptions, since they require evidence that is not already listed in the text. Explicit assumptions can be broken down into or supported by implicit assumptions.

Assumptions

Explicit Assumptions	Implicit Assumptions
A jazz club in Monroe would be profitable	• The jazz market is profitable • The club will make a substantial profit • The market size is sufficient to support the club
A jazz club in Monroe would have the market all to itself	• The main competitor is too distant to attract the Monroe population • The Monroe inhabitants that are going to the distant jazz club will choose C-Note based on proximity • There are no other competing jazz venues (cafes, bars etc.)
There is a big jazz fan base in Monroe	• The number of festival attendants accurately reflects the size of the market in Monroe • The rating of Jazz Nightly accurately reflects the popularity of jazz in Monroe • National survey reflects local preferences
Jazz fans will be willing to spend money on the club	• A great size of the average sums fans spend on jazz during the year will go into clubbing • Monroe's inhabitants can afford the club prices

After having established your assumptions, you can find the evidence that is needed to evaluate the argument by considering what proof is necessary to validate each implicit assumption.

Evidence

a) National jazz market statistics

b) C-Note's revenue and cash flow estimations compared with the costs of funding and operating the club.

c) Comparison of the minimum viable population necessary to support the club with the Monroe population (jazz market size)

d) Number of Monroe jazz fans frequenting the club situated 65 miles away from Monroe, reported to the size of the local jazz market

e) Number of jazz venues in the area

f) The percentage from the festival attendants that reside in Monroe

g) Jazz Nightly's audience ratings compared to Monroe's population size

h) The jazz radio's ratings compared to those of the competing stations

i) The percentage of money spent on clubbing from the estimated 1000 $ that the average jazz fan spends per year on jazz entertainment

j)   Monroe's income statistics reported to C-Note's ticket prices

k)   Comparison of the survey demographics with Monroe's demographics

Sample Essay

The authors of the loan application argue that a jazz club in Monroe would be profitable because the town boasts a big jazz fan base and the nearest competitor is located very far away. Before submitting the loan application, the group of developers would need to consider additional information, such as demographics, the competitor's prices, the real size of the Monroe jazz audience, and their willingness to spend money on jazz club entrance. Such an assessment would allow them to evaluate whether the business idea is viable in the first place.

The first bits of evidence that are lacking in the loan application are population statistics and their correlation with the club's funding and maintenance cost. The authors need to devise what are the minimum running costs and outline expected profit margins and couple those with the potential size of the jazz market in Monroe. This data should outline whether Monroe's jazz market size is sufficient to support the club. If Monroe's population is not great enough to meet the minimum viable population criteria, then the claim that a jazz club in Monroe would be profitable is not sustainable. Should the population criteria be met, the recommendation of building a jazz club in Monroe would garner some merit, but further data would be needed to establish the profitability of the club. For this purpose, the group of developers should compare C-Note's revenue and cash flow estimations with the costs of funding and operating the club. This would help to establish the theoretical financial viability of the Jazz club. The developers should keep in mind that in addition to these types of estimations, profitability is also highly dependent on the overall state of the market. As such, national jazz market statistics will showcase people's interest and willingness to spend money on jazz entertainment and paraphernalia. If the jazz market is under decline, as a National Endowment for the Arts study has discovered, a jazz club in Monroe might not be profitable in the long run. On the other hand, if the market shows signs of improvement, then the developer's propositions would be greatly strengthened by this fact.

The group of developers bases their business idea on Monroe having a big fan base for jazz. They justify their assumptions by providing a local jazz festival attendance rate and the popularity of the local jazz radio station. The information they provide is incomplete —the investors evaluating this application will not be able to see what percentage of the jazz festival attendants were locals. This data would help better showcase the size of Monroe's jazz market. If a great number of the attendants were local residents, then the assumption of a big jazz fan base in Monroe would be validated. If the data should reveal a low percentage of local residents from the total number of festival participants, then the claim of a large jazz fan base in Monroe would be weakened, which in turn will affect the expected profitability of the club. The group of developers brings another argument in favor of the popularity of jazz in Monroe, namely the ratings of the local jazz radio station. To verify if the rating of Jazz Nightly accurately reflects the popularity of jazz in Monroe, the developers would first need to report those ratings to the population of the town. This data would help them identify whether a significant part of the Monroe population listens to jazz, in which case their claims would be substantiated, or whether the radio listening people form just a small part of the population, in which case, the high radio ratings would not be indicative of the entire population's preferences.

When making their argument, the group of developers also assumes that a jazz club in Monroe will have the market all to itself because the nearest competitor is located at a great distance. To be able to establish whether this is the case, the loan applicants would have to compare C-Note and their competitor based on their prices, accessibility and reputation. By assessing what percentage of Monroe's jazz fan base frequents the club situated 65 miles away the investors can ascertain what part of the market already belongs to the competitor. In addition to this evidence, the developers should also provide data about the number of jazz venues in the area such as jazz cafes or bars, before concluding that the market would belong solely to the C-Note club. If indeed there are no other competitors in the area, C-note can enjoy market monopoly and the assumption that the club will be profitable becomes more plausible. However, should different jazz venues exist in the area, the developers would need to adjust their estimations and consider what size of the market belongs to the competitors and develop competitive strategies to be able to make the desired profits.

Another argument brought in to support the profitability of opening a jazz club in Monroe is a national survey that indicates the amounts of money the average jazz fan is willing to spend on jazz entertainment each year. To be able to assess how this information is related to the Monroe audience, the author would need to compare the survey demographics to those of the Monroe population. This data should be able to reveal whether the people of the survey are indicative for the jazz club's intended target audience, a fact which would make the survey findings applicable, or whether the two groups of people are radically different, in which case the survey would have no bearing on how the jazz fan base of Monroe would spend their money. Additionally, the authors should investigate what percentage of that money is spent for clubbing activities. Should it become evident that jazz fans like to spend a lot on clubs then that information would bode well for the future of C-Note. However, if the jazz fans in the study prefer to spend their money on different type of jazz events and paraphernalia, then the developers would need to provide additional data that would demonstrate that the people of Monroe would be willing to attend C-Note and develop good market and pricing strategies to bolster attendance.

All in all, the group of developers that argue for the profitability of opening a jazz club in Monroe stands a better chance of supporting their claim by providing a thorough market analysis coupled with a financial plan. They would stand a better chance at gaining a loan by providing a complete business plan and developing competitive strategies that would show that they can not only identify business opportunities but also know how to make the best of them.

Argument Task 9

Nature's Way, a chain of stores selling health food and other health-related products, is opening its next franchise in the town of Plainsville. The store should prove to be very successful: Nature's Way franchises tend to be most profitable in areas where residents lead healthy lives, and clearly Plainsville is such an area. Plainsville merchants report that sales of running shoes and exercise clothing are at all-time highs. The local health club has more members than ever, and the weight training and aerobics classes are always full. Finally, Plainsville's schoolchildren represent a new generation of potential customers: these schoolchildren are required to participate in a fitness-for-life program, which emphasizes the benefits of regular exercise at an early age.

Write a response in which you examine the stated and/or unstated assumptions of the argument. Be sure to explain how the argument depends on these assumptions and what the implications are for the argument if the assumptions prove unwarranted.

Strategies

Argument:

The argument uses information about healthful activities in Plainsville to support Nature's Way's opening its next franchise in Plainsville.

In developing your response to the topic, you must identify and examine both the stated and unstated assumptions of the argument to determine how the argument depends on those assumptions and how the argument fails if the assumptions prove to be incorrect.

Assumptions:

a) Nature's Way should be very successful in Plainsville. The writer assumes that the residents of Plainsville will purchase products from Nature's Way. This underlies the claim that Nature's Way will be successful in Plainsville. Since the residents are already health conscious, they may be buying health food somewhere else. Is there another health food store in Plainsville?

b) Nature's Way franchises tend to be profitable in areas where the residents lead healthy lives. "Tend" is a qualifying word; it is not absolute. Are some Nature's Way stores not profitable in areas where residents lead healthy lives? What might cause that lack of success?

c) The assumption that the children of Plainsville will be future customers of Nature's Way underlies the claim that Plainsville citizens lead healthy lives. There is no evidence that the children eat healthy food, just that they must participate in an exercise program. How many of these children will live in Plainsville as adults?

d) The residents of Plainsville lead healthy lives. The writer uses health club memberships and sales of running shoes and exercise clothing to support this assumption. It would be helpful to know how many of those club memberships are new and how many are renewals. How many times per week do the members go to the club to work out? What time of year is it? After the New Year's holiday, people make resolutions to lose weight, eat healthier, and exercise. Those resolutions rarely stick. The stores may be having after-Christmas sales, and the reduced prices have prompted the citizens to replace worn out sneakers and clothing.

Your notes do not have to be exhaustive. As you begin to write your essay, your brain will generate new ideas. Make certain that you keep the directions in mind as you develop your ideas.

Sample Essay

The writer of the passage has listed facts about the lifestyle of Plainsville residents that support the likely success of a Nature's Way franchise that is opening in that town. On the surface, this litany of healthy behaviors appears to be sufficient to bolster the position in the argument. Any good salesman would use a similar pitch to promote his product. However, several questions arise that could undermine the assumptions in this passage.

The first questions surround the reported increases in gym memberships and sales of sneakers and exercise clothing. It is no mystery that gym memberships increase at the beginning of each year. Adults make New Year's resolutions to lose weight, eat healthier food, and exercise more, resulting in upticks in the purchases of gym memberships, increased traffic at healthy food stores, and increased purchases of fitness clothing. After-holiday sales might also account for the increase in sales of sneakers and exercise clothing. After all, those new gym members need something to wear.

The argument also posits that future sales at Nature's Way are guaranteed as the children become healthier in Plainsville. They are required to participate in a program that emphasized the benefits of regular exercise at an early age. However, it is unclear whether this program requires them to exercise or eat healthy food, or how this might be enforced. Participation in the program does not guarantee participation in healthy activities. Their parents' food and exercise habits are more likely than a school program to influence the children's behavior. How many of those children will remain in Plainsville as adults? Merchants in other parts of the state or country are apt to benefit from the buying habits of these children when they become productive adults.

The assumption that any new business will be successful in any town is risky. Even Wal-Mart locations have failed in areas where the residents have no need to shop there. What is the median income in Plainsville? Are the residents college-educated? Specialty health-food stores cater to a relatively high socioeconomic group. Is there already a health-food store in Plainsville? What does Nature's Way have that will set it apart from businesses that already exist? Are the prices at Nature's Way low enough to attract a large customer base? Unless the store provides superior product or service, or a lower price point, it will not stand out in any appreciable way.

Finally, the author's use of the word *tend* should lead the reader to question the soundness of the assumptions in the passage. What happens to Nature's Way when it turns out that Plainsville residents don't stick to their resolutions to become healthier? They will find good excuses to skip going to the gym this week, and they'll rationalize their way through a pan of brownies. When all is said and done, the author's statement that Nature's Way should be successful may be correct. If the people of Plainsville are serious about leading healthy lives, they should shop at Nature's Way. That doesn't mean that they will.

Argument Task 10

> Fifteen years ago, Omega University implemented a new procedure that encouraged students to evaluate the teaching effectiveness of all their professors. Since that time, Omega professors have begun to assign higher grades in their classes, and overall student grade averages at Omega have risen by 30 percent. Potential employers, looking at this dramatic rise in grades, believe that grades at Omega are inflated and do not accurately reflect student achievement; as a result, Omega graduates have not been as successful at getting jobs as have graduates from nearby Alpha University. To enable its graduates to secure better jobs, Omega University should terminate student evaluation of professors.
>
> Write a response in which you discuss what specific evidence is needed to evaluate the argument and explain how the evidence would weaken or strengthen the argument.

Strategies

Argument:

This argument uses Omega graduates' difficulty obtaining jobs as a rationale for eliminating student evaluation of professors.

In developing your response, you must identify what specific evidence is needed to evaluate the writer's position and how that evidence weakens or strengthens that position.

What conclusions and assumptions are either explicit or implied in the argument?

Facts and Assumptions:

a) Student grade averages have risen by 30 percent at Omega University. This fact leads to the assumption that professors have inflated their students' grades. Over the course of 15 years, a number of changes could have occurred that can account for higher student grades. Has the school changed its admissions' policy? Has the school become more selective, admitting students with higher test scores and high school GPAs? It may be that professors have improved their instructional practices and/or material in response to the evaluations, and that has led to higher achievement.

b) Omega graduates have had less success getting jobs than graduates of nearby Alpha University. The assumption that follows this fact is that the inflated grades have created a negative impression about Omega students' real achievement. What courses of study does each school include? Perhaps Alpha University students have more desirable or marketable skills.

c) Omega University instituted student evaluation of professors fifteen years ago. This fact led to the assumption that professors began inflating grades, ostensibly to receive better evaluations from students. Why did Omega U initiate this policy? Who evaluated the professors prior to this? What effect on professors do the survey results have? Do the results affect tenure? Retention? Remediation? What is the content of the evaluations?

d) Omega University grades have risen by 30 percent, which has led to the assumption that professors have inflated student grades.

Your notes do not have to be exhaustive. As you begin to write your essay, your brain will generate new ideas. Make certain that you keep the directions in mind as you develop your ideas.

Sample Essay

Employers have interpreted the rise in grades for Omega University graduates as an indication that professors are awarding higher marks in response to the institution's use of student evaluation. As a result, Omega graduates have more difficulty finding jobs than do the graduates of nearby Alpha University. In response to this unfortunate consequence, the writer posits that Omega University should terminate student evaluation of professors. If there is substantive evidence for this change, it has not been revealed in the passage.

Employers assume that professors have inflated grades to receive favorable evaluations from their students. Employers might benefit from knowing what aspects of the professors' pedagogy are evaluated. It may be that, over the fifteen-year period that student evaluations have existed, professors have responded by improving their instructional techniques and curriculum materials. In consequence, students have found the classes more relevant and accessible and have had greater success than previous students. It is also unclear whether the evaluations of the professors have improved with the increase in grades. If it has not, this argument is invalid.

Another assumption that needs to be examined is that the quality of students has remained steady while grades have risen. Can evidence be uncovered that reveals a change in Omega University's admissions policy? The school may have instituted more stringent admissions requirements. The cohorts may have achieved higher scores on the SAT or taken Advanced Placement courses in high school. Omega University's increased selectivity could account for a rise in grades. It might be helpful to know if the student evaluation process replaced another type of evaluation. It could be that the professors, themselves, requested the student evaluation to help them critique their own effectiveness.

Finally, we must look at the 30 percent rise in grades. The reader may interpret this to mean that all of Omega University students have raised their GPA's or their actual numerical averages by 30 percent. Assuming that a student would need at least a 70 percent average to remain in school, a 30 percent increase would mean that every student has a minimum average of 91 percent. That would, indeed, be remarkable and a likely cause for skepticism on the parts of employers. However, if the statistic means that 30 percent of Omega students have increased their grade averages, it may not be a cause for concern. If Omega University has 1,000 students, then roughly 300 of them have raised their grades, a more realistic improvement. Employers should not write off these graduates without understanding the basis of the purported elevation of grades.

Omega University graduates' inability to secure employment may be due, in part, to suspicion about their actual achievement, but other factors may contribute to the dearth of jobs for them. Alpha University may offer majors in courses of study that are more marketable in today's economy.

Argument Task 11

> The council of Maple County, concerned about the county's becoming overdeveloped, is debating a proposed measure that would prevent the development of existing farmland in the county. But the council is also concerned that such a restriction, by limiting the supply of new housing, could lead to significant increases in the price of housing in the county. Proponents of the measure note that Chestnut County established a similar measure ten years ago and its housing prices have increased only modestly since. However, opponents of the measure note that Pine County adopted restrictions on the development of new residential housing fifteen years ago, and its housing prices have since more than doubled. The council currently predicts that the proposed measure, if passed, will result in a significant increase in housing prices in Maple County.
>
> Write a response in which you discuss what questions would need to be answered in order to decide whether the prediction and the argument on which it is based are reasonable. Be sure to explain how the answers to these questions would help to evaluate the prediction.

Strategies

Prediction:

Limiting the development of existing farmland will result in a significant increase in housing prices in Maple County.

Argument:

Proponents point to a similar measure's being adopted in Chestnut County resulting in only a modest increase in housing prices. Opponents point to a similar measure's being adopted in Pine County resulting in housing prices more than doubling.

Questions:

a) What is the median income in each of the other counties? How do they compare to the median income in Maple County?

b) How do the school systems in the three counties compare?

c) What was the housing inventory in the other two counties prior to development? What is the housing inventory in Maple County? This would include apartments, condominiums, town houses, as well as detached single-family homes.

d) What incentive is there for people to move to any of the three counties? The counties may provide different services and facilities that make one county more desirable than the others.

e) Is one of the counties home to a large city? Development around a large urban area may demand higher prices.

f) What is the demographic of each county? It could be that Pine County residents are married couples with two incomes and growing families who need larger homes. Chestnut County residents may be retirees who are downsizing.

g)   Is there anything inherently wrong with increased prices for homes in Maple County? The residents of Maple County may benefit from a rise in real estate prices. The council may fear that higher housing prices will discourage people from moving to their county.

Your notes do not have to be exhaustive. As you begin to write your essay, your brain will generate new ideas. Make certain that you keep the directions in mind as you develop your ideas.

Sample Essay

In a backlash against urban sprawl, counties have created restrictions and parameters for development that requires expanding their infrastructure and broadening the scope of their services. When a developer presents a plan for a new residential subdivision, he relies on the community to extend its water and sewer lines and lay down new streets. There are more structures for the fire department to cover, more area for police cruisers to patrol, and more roadways for plows to clear in winter. If families with children move into the new homes, the schools may become overcrowded. The expansion of the tax base may not offset increased costs to the city. Despite these additional demands, an expanded housing inventory tends to keep prices affordable and encourages people to move to the area. The council of Maple County would be wise to consider several questions before deciding either course of action regarding development.

The main objection to restricting development appears to be a fear that housing prices will increase dramatically. This is a likely consequence only if conditions that exist in Maple County are similar to those in Pine County. Why did housing prices more than double in Pine County? It may be that Pine County is a more desirable place to live, and there is a greater demand for homes there. Supply and demand always influence the price of any commodity. Pine County may be home to a large city that provides great career opportunities and cultural activities that make its suburbs attractive to upper middle-class citizens. Pine County may have award-winning schools that attract young families desiring a high-quality education for their children. If Pine County does, indeed, possess these attributes, a lack of housing inventory would inflate the prices of existing homes.

In contrast, Chestnut County may lack the desirable characteristics that make an area attractive to people seeking a new place to live. Why did the prices of homes in Chestnut County experience only a moderate increase when officials limited development there? This county may be rural in nature, with significant distances between homes, eliminating the neighborhood structure that families find appealing. It may be that Chestnut County lacks opportunities for shopping, recreation, and cultural activities that attract well-educated, affluent families. Its schools may not be stellar, discouraging families with children from settling there. Even though Chestnut County has limited housing inventory, the demand for the homes that do exist simply isn't as high as it is in Pine County. As a result, any increases in prices there are likely due to inflation.

How does Maple County settle the argument about restricting development? Members of the council should complete a thorough analysis of the three counties to determine how Maple County is similar to or different from the other two. If Maple County has more in common with Pine County, they may want to lift restrictions on development and allow more homes to be built to keep housing prices affordable. On the other hand, if Maple County has more in common with Chestnut County, restricting development for the time being may be the wisest course. They will not have expended county funds to expand infrastructure and services for a county that is not likely to attract sufficient numbers of new residents to offset the cost of such improvement.

Argument Task 12

> *The following appeared in a memorandum from the manager of WWAC radio station.*
>
> *"To reverse a decline in listener numbers, our owners have decided that WWAC must change from its current rock-music format. The decline has occurred despite population growth in our listening area, but that growth has resulted mainly from people moving here after their retirement. We must make listeners of these new residents. We could switch to a music format tailored to their tastes, but a continuing decline in local sales of recorded music suggests limited interest in music. Instead we should change to a news and talk format, a form of radio that is increasingly popular in our area."*
>
> Write a response in which you discuss what specific evidence is needed to evaluate the argument and explain how the evidence would weaken or strengthen the argument.

NOTE: The above topic has wording similar to Argument Task 26 of GRE Analytical Writing Solution to the Real Essay Topics - Book 2. However, if you read carefully you will notice that the task instructions are different. Hence, it is very important to read the topic as well as its instructions completely before you start to write your response.

Strategies

Argument:

This argument uses a decline in listener numbers as justification for changing the radio station's format.

In developing your response, you are asked to identify what specific evidence is needed to evaluate the strength of the argument and explain how the evidence supports or negates the argument.

Facts and Assumptions:

a) The fact is that there has been a decline in listener numbers. This leads to the assumption that the station needs to revise its format. Which demographic has caused this decline? Is the decline sudden, or has it happened over a period of years? Are other stations in the area experiencing a similar decline in listeners?

b) Local sales of recorded music have declined causing the station owners to assume that there is limited interest in music. Why has the sale of record music declined? Does the local store maintain sufficient inventory that includes a wide variety of genres? Has a dip in the general economy of the area contributed to the lack of sales? Has the radio station surveyed the local population to determine what type of music, if any, it is interested in? Has the growth of MP3 players affected the sales of recorded music? Satellite radio has changed the way people listen to music.

c) The decline in listener numbers has led the owners to assume that a news and talk format would attract new listeners. Have the owners conducted a survey to determine if this is the case? If other stations are using this format, is the market saturated?

d) The station owners have assumed that, since the rock-music format has lost its popularity, no other music genre should take its place.

Your notes do not have to be exhaustive. As you begin to write your essay, your brain will generate new ideas. Make certain that you keep the directions in mind as you develop your ideas.

Sample Essay

The station manager has assumed that a decline in listener numbers should lead to a change in format at WWAC. This is an executive decision based on lack of concrete evidence. He or she must find out why listeners are abandoning the station before making any drastic changes that could further alienate listeners.

The station manager contradicts the impact of the population growth in the area. On one hand, he implies that population growth should create more listeners, but, on the other hand, implies that, because most of the new residents are retirees, he doesn't expect them to become fans of the current format anyway. Despite that, he wants to make listeners of them and feels that changing the format will do the trick. This could very well alienate the station's faithful listeners.

This manager associates the low sales of recorded music with a decline in his station's listeners. He further assumes that people have a limited interest in music overall. The popularity of MP3 players contradicts this assumption. One only has to walk down the halls of any high school or the streets of any city to observe this phenomenon. People are going about their daily routines with wires trailing from earbuds that keep them tuned in. The online music store, iTunes, is doing a brisk business, and one can preview and buy music from the comfort of home. Satellite radio has cornered a portion of the listeners, as well. New cars come equipped with satellite receivers, and satellite dishes attached to homes in every neighborhood bring every genre of music imaginable into homes across the country. Those satellite connections and cable television may deliver several stations devoted to news and talk shows.

Local brick-and-mortar radio stations face many challenges. They, indeed, may have to make some format adjustments, not only to attract new listeners, but to keep the ones that they have. This manager should discover the demographic of the area. Does one particular culture dominate? Does a large portion of the population speak Spanish or French? Are there a number of devotees of opera or classical music? It could be that the station doesn't offer enough variety. Switching to a talk format would still make WWAC a one-note station. If the manager is basing his decision on the popularity of talk shows already being broadcast in the area, is he moving into a market that is already saturated? It certainly won't make WWAC stand out among its competitors.

WWAC's manager may need to revisit what has worked for the station in the past. When were its listener numbers the greatest? What was the station doing at that time? Was it running a promotion? Were listeners able to call in and make requests for special songs? When did listener numbers begin to decline? Has the decline been gradual or sudden? Are other stations experiencing the same phenomenon? At the very least, the station manager should conduct a survey of resident's in the station's broadcast range to find out their ages, interests, and tastes in music. If he tunes his listeners out, they won't tune in to WWAC.

Argument Task 13

> *The following is a memorandum from the business manager of a television station.*
>
> *"Over the past year, our late-night news program has devoted increased time to national news and less time to weather and local news. During this period, most of the complaints received from viewers were concerned with our station's coverage of weather and local news. In addition, local businesses that used to advertise during our late-night news program have canceled their advertising contracts with us. Therefore, in order to attract more viewers to our news programs and to avoid losing any further advertising revenues, we should expand our coverage of weather and local news on all our news programs."*
>
> Write a response in which you examine the stated and/or unstated assumptions of the argument. Be sure to explain how the argument depends on these assumptions and what the implications are for the argument if the assumptions prove unwarranted.

NOTE: *The above topic has wording similar to Argument Task 8 of GRE Analytical Writing Solution to the Real Essay Topics - Book 2. However, if you read carefully you will notice that the task instructions are different. Hence, it is very important to read the topic as well as its instructions completely before you start to write your response.*

Strategies

Argument:

Based on a decline in listener numbers, the business manager of a television station has recommended expanding coverage of weather and local news on all of its news programs.

In developing your response, you must examine the stated and/or unstated assumptions of the argument and how the soundness of the argument relies on them.

Facts and Assumptions:

a) Over the past year, the station has devoted increased time to national news and less time to weather and local news. The assumption is that the station was responding to viewer demand. An additional assumption might be that it's easier to hook up to a national news feed than to produce a local news broadcast.

b) During that time, customers complained about the station's coverage of weather and local news. Based on the previous statement, one might assume that customers want more coverage. However, customers may be unhappy with the time slot devoted to local news. Customers may simply not like the newscasters. They also may be complaining about lack of accuracy in the weather forecast. Most of the complaints are about news and weather. What are the other complaints?

c) Local businesses have canceled advertising contracts for the late-night news broadcast. It would be easy to assume that advertisers are expressing their displeasure with the late-night news show. On the other hand, they may have shifted their advertising dollars to other time slots. They may have had to make some economic decisions about advertising dollars.

d) Expanding local news and weather on all of the station's news programs will prevent the loss of further advertising revenues. The business manager may be incorrectly assuming that this is the only point of dissatisfaction with the station.

Your notes do not have to be exhaustive. As you begin to write your essay, your brain will generate new ideas. Make certain that you keep the directions in mind as you develop your ideas.

Sample Essay

Television is facing stiffer competition than ever before in its history. New cable stations are popping up seemingly every day. In consequence, businesses are faced with deciding how to spend their advertising dollars. Do they maintain their focus on local stations or spread the money around on the cable networks that their customers also watch? The manager of the local television station is under the illusion that complaints about local news and weather coverage are his only problem. Maintaining that illusion could lead him to make some fatal decisions.

Attracting more viewers may attract more advertising dollars. However, the assumption that increasing weather and local news coverage is the means to attract these viewers it may be erroneous. Has the business manager spoken with his advertisers to find out why they cancelled their contracts? They could be looking for a better price or desire exclusivity in their time slot. The advertisers may not like the sound or graphics that the station uses in their ads. There are many other potential reasons why these contracts were cancelled that have little to do with the station's approach to news coverage.

A second assumption arises from viewer complaints. Since most of the complaints are about weather and local news coverage, the manager has decided to increase coverage of both on all of the station's news shows. The viewers might dislike the newscasters or desire more accuracy in the weather report. The television might be in the middle of farm country where accurate and frequent weather reports have a significant impact on planting and harvesting schedules. The business manager needs more details about the full nature of the viewer complaints. Those viewers may not be concerned about the amount of news coverage but by the content. They might appreciate more human-interest stories or segments about health or high school sports. The business manager's thinking may be too narrow in scope. The economy of the area may be experiencing a downturn. Advertisers' canceling contracts may have nothing to do with programming and everything to do with their own bottom lines. Has the station manager considered discounting the advertising rates in an effort entice the deserters to return? The economy may be contributing to the number of viewer complaints. More residents may be unemployed and watching more television. As a result, they are more aware of what is happening on their local television station.

The business manager may mistakenly assume that he can do anything to remedy the situation he finds himself in. The network that the station broadcasts may have an unpopular lineup of shows, and stations affiliated with that network around the county are in the same position. This is beyond the business manager's control unless he can convince the owners to apply to another major network.

Argument Task 14

The following appeared in an article written by Dr. Karp, an anthropologist.

"Twenty years ago, Dr. Field, a noted anthropologist, visited the island of Tertia and concluded from his observations that children in Tertia were reared by an entire village rather than by their own biological parents. However, my recent interviews with children living in the group of islands that includes Tertia show that these children spend much more time talking about their biological parents than about other adults in the village. This research of mine proves that Dr. Field's conclusion about Tertian village culture is invalid and thus that the observation-centered approach to studying cultures is invalid as well. The interview-centered method that my team of graduate students is currently using in Tertia will establish a much more accurate understanding of child-rearing traditions there and in other island cultures."

Write a response in which you discuss what specific evidence is needed to evaluate the argument and explain how the evidence would weaken or strengthen the argument.

Strategies

Argument:

The interview-centered method will establish a more accurate understanding of child- rearing traditions in Tertiary than did the observation- centered approach.

In developing your response, you are asked to identify specific evidence that Dr. Karp needs to sustain the validity of his position.

Facts and Assumptions:

a)   Twenty years ago, Dr. Field observed that children in Tertia were reared by an entire village rather than by their own biological parents.

b)   Recently, Dr. Karp visited the group of islands that includes Tertia and used the interview-centered method to study child-rearing practices. Readers of this passage might assume that he interviewed residents of Tertia to compare practices from twenty years ago to those of today.

c)   The children interviewed by Dr. Karp spent more time talking about their biological parents than other adults in the village. The assumption is that child- rearing practices may have changed over the last twenty years or that Dr. Field's conclusions were incorrect.

d)   Dr. Karp did conclude that Dr. Field's conclusions must be invalid. The assumption is that Dr. Karp's methods yield more accurate results.

Questions:

a) Why did Dr. Field choose the observation-center method to study the people of Tertia? Did he have good results with that method in previous studies?

b) What prompted Dr. Karp to visit this group of islands? Did he actually visit and interview the residents of Tertia?

c) What types of questions did Dr. Karp use with the children he interviewed? Did he ask them about all adults, or did he restrict his questions to those about their parents?

d) Have child-rearing practices changed in the twenty years between the two visits?

Your notes do not have to be exhaustive. As you begin to write your essay, your brain will generate new ideas. Make certain that you keep the directions in mind as you develop your ideas.

Sample Essay

Ever since Margaret Mead journeyed to study the Samoans in the early part of the twentieth century, anthropologists have continued to investigate the social mores of remote groups around the world. Each anthropologist is bound to have a preferred method for confuting research, and they may alternate those methods depending on what aspect of the culture they are investigating. To evaluate Dr. Karp's recommendation, the reader requires evidence that his interview-centered method is superior to Dr. Field's observation-centered approach.

The first piece of evidence should reveal the purpose of each anthropologist's visit to the area of Tertia. It is not even clear that Dr. Karp actually visited Tertia itself. The passage implies that each of them purposely studied child-rearing practices since no mention is made of other results. However, it could be that those results are ancillary to the real purpose of each visit. The studies may have had a broader scope than is revealed in this passage. In addition, if Dr. Karp pursued this study in reaction to the data he saw from Dr. Field's work, he may have made assumptions about the study's conclusions that would bias his experimental design.

Dr. Karp currently has a team of graduate students using the interview-based method to study child- rearing practices in Tertia. The content of an interview can be designed to elicit specific types of responses. Do the questions lead the children of Tertia to talk about their parents rather than other adults on the island? There is a world of difference between asking, "When do your parents feed you?" and "When do you eat your meals?" Are the graduate students using questions developed by Dr. Karp, or have they created their own questions? Grad students may not have enough experience to write questions that are objective.

Twenty years have passed since Dr. Field visited and observed the residents of Tertia. Is there evidence of any outside influences on village life since his visit? The rapid growth of technology has created the global village, and it is difficult to imagine that Tertia has not been, at least tangentially, affected. Satellites have made access to the World Wide Web possible from virtually anywhere on the globe. Cellular phones are ubiquitous. It is even possible that Dr. Field's visit, itself, influenced the behavior of the Tertians. In fact, it would be unrealistic to believe that child-rearing practices have remained static anywhere.

The one piece of evidence that is clear is that Dr. Karp wrote the article. It is doubtful that this anthropologist has maintained an objective point of view while contrasting the two research methods. An opinion delivered by a scientist with no vested interest in the outcome might be the strongest evidence for evaluating the strength of the argument.

Argument Task 15

> *According to a recent report, cheating among college and university students is on the rise. However, Groveton College has successfully reduced student cheating by adopting an honor code, which calls for students to agree not to cheat in their academic endeavors and to notify a faculty member if they suspect that others have cheated. Groveton's honor code replaced a system in which teachers closely monitored students; under that system, teachers reported an average of thirty cases of cheating per year. In the first year the honor code was in place, students reported twenty-one cases of cheating; five years later, this figure had dropped to fourteen. Moreover, in a recent survey, a majority of Groveton students said that they would be less likely to cheat with an honor code in place than without. Thus, all colleges and universities should adopt honor codes similar to Groveton's in order to decrease cheating among students.*
>
> Write a response in which you discuss what questions would need to be answered in order to decide whether the recommendation and the argument on which it is based are reasonable. Be sure to explain how the answers to these questions would help to evaluate the recommendation.

NOTE: The above topic has wording similar to Argument Task 7 of GRE Analytical Writing Solution to the Real Essay Topics - Book 1. However, if you read carefully you will notice that the task instructions are different. Hence, it is very important to read the topic as well as its instructions completely before you start to write your response.

Strategies

Argument:

The writer recommends that all colleges and universities adopt an honor code similar to Groveton's.

In developing your response, you are directed to discuss what questions need to be answered before other colleges accept this recommendation.

Begin by identifying the facts and assumptions in the passage.

Facts and Assumptions:

a) Cheating among college students is increasing. This reported fact should lead colleges to take some action to curtail cheating. The assumption accompanying this fact is that Groveton's policy provides the means to achieve this.

b) Groveton has successfully reduced cheating. The writer assumes that this is a result of the honor code.

c) The current honor code replaced teacher monitoring of students. The reader might assume that teacher monitoring became ineffective or burdensome. The administration may have wanted students to take more responsibility for their own learning.

d) Under the old system, professors reported an average of 30 cases of cheating per year. The reader should assume that in some years there were more cases of cheating, and, in other years, there were fewer than thirty cases.

e)   In the first year of the newer policy, students reported 21 cases of cheating. The assumption is that there was less cheating immediately following adoption of the new policy. It is better than the previous practice.

f)   Five years after adopting the new policy, there were 14 cases of cheating. The assumption is that there has been a steady decline in the number of cheating cases. This assumption supports the administration's adoption of the new policy.

g)   Students report that they are less likely to cheat with an honor code in place. The reader assumes that an honor code is the best way to prevent or decrease the incidence of cheating.

Questions:

a)   Why do college students cheat? Which students cheat? Some student may feel greater pressure to achieve at a high level at some colleges. Students may have heavy, challenging course loads that prevent them from completing their work unless they cheat.

b)   Why did Groveton adopt an honor code to replace teacher monitoring? Whose idea was it? Was the change based on research?

c)   How many cases of cheating were there every year that the teachers monitored the students? What was the low number? The high number?

d)   How many cases of cheating were reported in years 2, 3, and 4 of the new system? There may have been enough cases to create an average similar to that of the old system.

e)   Why do students say they are less likely to cheat with an honor code in place? What questions were they asked? Were they asked if they prefer an honor code to teacher monitoring?

Considering how these questions might be answered will help you to evaluate the soundness of the recommendation.

Your notes do not have to be exhaustive. As you begin to write your essay, your brain will generate new ideas. Make certain that you keep the directions in mind as you develop your ideas.

Sample Essay

Why do students cheat? They do it at every level: elementary school through college and from the most gifted to the most challenged students. How does a school prevent cheating on the part of its students? Groveton College claims to have created a tool that decreases the number of cheating incidents by students on its campus. At Groveton College, students essentially monitor themselves by adhering to a recently instituted honor code. Under this system, students agree to avoid cheating and to report suspected cases of cheating to a faculty member. Before another college adopts Groveton's policy, the administration should ask why Groveton changed from its former practice of having teachers closely monitor their students. Is there some academic research that proves the efficacy of honor codes and peer reporting? Has Groveton responded to a petition by either or both its teachers and students?

The reported decline in the number of reported cheating incidents seems impressive on the surface. Another college looking at these statistics may agree that an honor code is the policy to create on its own campus. That school would be advised to look further into the numbers. The report cited reveals an average number of cases reported when teachers were monitoring students but omits a yearly average for the years since the honor code has been in place. During the first year of the new practice, students reported twenty-one cases of cheating, and in the most recent year only fourteen cases. It would be easy to assume that there has been a steady decline in cheating at Groveton College. What were the numbers during the intervening years? It is possible that those numbers, when added to the first and last years' totals could average thirty, the same yearly average under the old system of monitoring.

Groveton has taken the additional step of surveying its students about the effectiveness of the new honor code. Students report that they are less likely to cheat with an honor code in place than without. Did the survey ask about other practices used to curtail cheating? Is an honor code preferable because the consequences are less severe? Did Groveton change the consequences for cheating when it allowed students to self report? It is entirely possible that this response is biased by a fear of negative consequences resulting from cheating, making students unwilling to admit their true propensity to do so.

Colleges and universities agonize over the amount of cheating on their campuses. In response to the report that says cheating is on the rise, a college or university may be willing to try anything that appears to have some success. Reporting incidents of cheating is similar to closing the barn door after the horse has escaped. The cheating has already occurred. Any institution of higher learning might be better served by discovering why students cheat. Are the course loads and work requirements too cumbersome? Is there too much pressure to succeed at a high level? Is there too much competition to be admitted to graduate school or to get a good job? Society itself may have created an environment conducive to cheating by demanding that its college graduates be the best and the brightest.

Before accepting the recommendation to adopt Groveton's honor code, other colleges and universities should demand more information and scrutinize the practices that they have in place. Perhaps the best course of action is stopping cheating before it occurs. An ounce of prevention is worth a pound of cure.

Argument Task 16

> The following appeared in a memorandum from the planning department of an electric power company.
>
> "Several recent surveys indicate that home owners are increasingly eager to conserve energy. At the same time, manufacturers are now marketing many home appliances, such as refrigerators and air conditioners, that are almost twice as energy efficient as those sold a decade ago. Also, new technologies for better home insulation and passive solar heating are readily available to reduce the energy needed for home heating. Therefore, the total demand for electricity in our area will not increase - and may decline slightly. Since our three electric generating plants in operation for the past twenty years have always met our needs, construction of new generating plants will not be necessary.
>
> Write a response in which you examine the stated and/or unstated assumptions of the argument. Be sure to explain how the argument depends on these assumptions and what the implications are for the argument if the assumptions prove unwarranted.

Strategies

Argument:

Because of the availability of energy-saving appliances and new technology for better home insulation and heating, the current power plants will not need to be replaced.

In developing your response, you are asked to examine the stated and unstated assumptions in the argument and explain how the arguments depend on the assumptions' soundness to sustain the argument.

Facts and Assumptions:

a) Surveys show that home owners are increasingly eager to conserve energy. The assumption derived from this fact is that the home owners will conserve energy and will take steps to make that possible.

b) Many manufacturers are producing home appliances that are almost twice as energy-efficient as those sold a decade ago. The writer assumes that consumers, in an effort to reduce their energy consumption, will buy these new appliances. Appliances are a big expense. How long will it take the home owners to recoup the cost of the appliances through energy savings? Homeowners are likely to keep a new appliance for more than ten years, so if they bought their current inefficient appliances just before manufacturers changed their designs, they may not be ready for new ones.

c) New technologies exist for better home insulation and passive solar heating. Again, the writer assumes that home owners are going to install new insulation or passive solar heating devices. The cost/return factor may come into play here, as well.

d) The total demand for electricity in the area will not increase. This assumes that no new factories will be built and that no new residents will move to the area. Every existing condition would have to remain the same for demand for electricity to remain the same.

e) The current three electricity-generating plants have served the needs of the area for twenty years and will not have to be replaced. The assumption here is that these twenty-year-old plants have technology that will continue to produce electricity efficiently. Again, this assumption is based on zero-population growth and industry and business remaining what it is today.

Your notes do not have to be exhaustive. As you begin to write your essay, your brain will generate new ideas. Make certain that you keep the directions in mind as you develop your ideas.

Sample Essay

This memorandum claims that there is no need to construct more electric plants due to an increased interest from the local population in energy conservation. The claims in this memorandum rely on several assumptions being correct, and the writer uses some facts about energy use in the area to support these assumptions. This writer is also relying on the behavior of others to make a recommendation for the future of the electric company. In reality, the only behavior one can predict is his own.

Building a new electricity-generating plant is expensive and time- consuming. Most companies would rather avoid having to do so. The writer in this case appears to have done some research to support his proposition that the three existing plants will be sufficient into the future. The first fact derives from a survey that reports home owners' desires to conserve energy. The writer does not say how homeowners plan to accomplish that, nor does it reveal in which areas they want to save that energy. Do they want to reduce their electricity usage, or cut back on the amount of heating fuel they consume? They may decide to install a wood or pellet stove to heat their homes instead of reducing their electricity use.

The writer goes on to cite the move on the parts of manufactures to produce and market more energy-efficient appliances as a rationale for maintaining the status quo. It is probably true in every case, that, when consumers today shop for new appliances, they look for the energy star and nod with satisfaction when buying a refrigerator that uses only $60.00 worth of electricity each year. In calculating their savings, they must determine how many years it will take to recoup the cost of that new refrigerator, which, in most cases, will cost upwards of $1000. If the benefit isn't great enough, they may postpone that purchase. Those building new homes may opt for those new appliances, but the planning department would need to know how much of their total energy usage is demanded by new construction. In addition, new technologies in the insulation and passive solar heating sector have encouraged the planning department to estimate less or static energy demand from their current generators. Retrofitting older homes to take advantage of these new technologies is expensive, and homeowners will once again calculate the cost/savings ratio before making those changes. Passive solar technology is only effective in an area with sufficient sunlight. Is that true of the area where this energy company operates?

After considering the availability of appliances and technologies available to consumers who want to reduce their energy use, the planning committee has concluded that energy use will not increase and may even decline in the future. This conclusion precludes any type of growth in the area. For energy use to remain static, no new factories or homes could be built. In contradiction to this idea is the likelihood that local town and city planners are recruiting new businesses and families to move to their communities.

The final solution proposed by the planning department is to forego any plans for a new power plant and to remain with the three existing plants that have served them well for the past twenty years. This proposal relies on the assumptions' having sound foundations and the lack of growth in the area. To presume that twenty-year-old machinery will not need upgrading or replacing could lead to unsound financial decision on the part of the power company. The charge this writer should be making to the power company is to act prudently and plan for future growth.

Argument Task 17

> *The vice president of human resources at Climpson Industries sent the following recommendation to the company's president.*
>
> *"In an effort to improve our employees' productivity, we should implement electronic monitoring of employees' Internet use from their workstations. Employees who use the Internet from their workstations need to be identified and punished if we are to reduce the number of work hours spent on personal or recreational activities, such as shopping or playing games. By installing software to detect employees' Internet use on company computers, we can prevent employees from wasting time, foster a better work ethic at Climpson, and improve our overall profits."*
>
> Write a response in which you examine the stated and/or unstated assumptions of the argument. Be sure to explain how the argument depends on these assumptions and what the implications are for the argument if the assumptions prove unwarranted.

Strategies

Argument:

Monitoring employees' Internet use will improve productivity by keeping them from wasting time on personal and recreational activities. The result will be increased company profits.

Assumptions:

a) Climpson Industries has assumed that its employees are using the Internet for personal business. How did this suspicion arise? Has Climpson heard this complaint from other businesses?

b) They have also assumed that personal Internet use has caused a loss in productivity. If employees are not as productive as the company would like, there may be reasons other than Internet use. Does the company provide ongoing training? Incentives for increased productivity?

c) Monitoring Internet use will improve company profits.

d) Employees are wasting time. Is there sufficient meaningful work to keep them busy throughout the work day?

e) Employees have a poor work ethic. Has this been demonstrated by employees' arriving late for work or leaving early? Do they call in sick on a regular basis?

f) Punishment will increase productivity. This is rarely the case. Positive reinforcement or incentives are more likely to increase productivity. Employees need to know what's in it for them. Punishment is generally a short-term solution.

Your notes do not have to be exhaustive. As you begin to write your essay, your brain will generate new ideas. Make certain that you keep the directions in mind as you develop your ideas.

Sample Essay

Climpson Industries, to improve its overall profits, is proposing to monitor its employees' Internet use. Although there appears to be no concrete evidence, the company assumes that its employees are wasting time on the Internet for personal and recreational activities during work hours. The vice president of human resources is suggesting a Big Brother approach to ensure that company employees are doing what they're supposed to be doing in the workplace.

The company assumes that its employees are using the Internet for personal and recreational activities. Simply asking the employees about Internet use may be more efficacious than assuming the worst? Done in a respectful and professional manner, an interview with each employee may confirm or belay the company's suspicions. A lack of productivity would result in deadlines being missed or orders being left unfilled. Is that happening at Climpson? If not, then current productivity is not in question. If the company seeks to improve productivity, it would do so in response to an increased demand for its products or services.

In conjunction with the assumed lack of productivity is the belief that employees are wasting time. Do the employees have enough meaningful work to fill their days? If current quotas are being met, the employees must be working efficiently. If they have time to waste, it is because their time is not filled by employer demands. The additional assumption of a poor work ethic would also be reflected in work going undone. Employees with a poor work ethic are apt to call in sick, arrive late to work, take extended lunch breaks, and/or leave early at the end of the day. If such behavior exists at Climpson Industries, it would be blatantly obvious and easy to check by reviewing time cards.

The desire to punish the slackers on the company payroll is counterproductive. What form would the punishment take that would not have deleterious consequences for the company itself? It would, in the long term, cause discontent and dissatisfaction with the managers. Knowledgeable and profitable employers know that incentives are a more effective means of increasing productivity and employee loyalty. In turn, company profits are likely to increase.

The changes in technology over the past couple of decades have created new challenges for business. A proactive approach would be to adopt policies before implementing changes. Does Climpson Industries have a policy manual that outlines what are and are not acceptable activities regarding Internet use? When the rules are clear, employees will generally have no trouble obeying them. Rather than taking on the role of Big Brother, the management would be better served by acting as coaches and leading their employees and, concomitantly, their company to greater success.

Argument Task 18

> The following appeared in a memorandum from the owner of Movies Galore, a chain of movie-rental stores.
>
> "Because of declining profits, we must reduce operating expenses at Movies Galore's ten movie-rental stores. Raising prices is not a good option, since we are famous for our low prices. Instead, we should reduce our operating hours. Last month our store in downtown Marston reduced its hours by closing at 6:00 p.m. rather than 9:00 p.m. and reduced its overall inventory by no longer stocking any DVD released more than five years ago. Since we have received very few customer complaints about these new policies, we should now adopt them at all other Movies Galore stores as our best strategies for improving profits."
>
> Write a response in which you discuss what specific evidence is needed to evaluate the argument and explain how the evidence would weaken or strengthen the argument.

Strategies

A good place to start your analysis is by creating a statement that reveals the main idea of the argument. Although the writer is creating an argument, he may ultimately be stating a position, making a recommendation, or making a prediction. It may be helpful for you to determine which of these formats is most evident in the argument.

The owner of Movies Galore predicts that cost-saving measures taken at the downtown Marston location will prove successful in his other stores and sees reducing hours as preferable to increasing their famously low prices.

Assumptions:

a) Reducing operating expenses will increase profits.

b) Raising prices will have a negative effect on Movie Galore's reputation.

c) What has worked for the downtown Marston store will work in the other locations.

d) Measures taken in the downtown Marston store have increased profits.

e) Customers have adapted to the changes in the downtown store.

f) Customers choose Movies Galore because of its low price.

g) The owner can make changes that will affect the stores' profitability.

Evidence needed to evaluate the argument:

a) How other operating expenses have increased or decreased in the years that Movies Galore has been in operation?

b) How Movie Galore's prices compare to those of other similar businesses?

c) Why people shop at Movies Galore?

d)   How the changes at the downtown Marston store have affected its profitability?

e)   Customer count before and after the changes in downtown Marston store.

f)   What times of the day are busiest?

g)   How services such as Netflix or Red Box and the availability of cable or satellite stations affect movies Galore?

After completing these steps, you should have enough material to write your analysis. Remember that you are not creating a position of your own; you are evaluating the strengths and weaknesses of the existing argument. You do not have to include all of the points that you have created in your prewriting. In fact, during the process of drafting your analysis, other ideas may come to mind, and, if they strengthen your analysis, you should include them.

Sample Essay

Declining profits are a concern for any business, and Movies Galore is no exception. The owner of this chain of stores has taken some steps in the downtown Marston location that he believes should be applied at the other locations to reduce expenses and increase profits. Before rushing to judgment, this owner should evaluate several factors. Without sufficient evidence, he or she may make a fatal mistake.

It may be that the type of inventory and length of the business day contribute to the lack of profitability, but other operating expenses must not be overlooked. The owner must examine fixed expenses such as utilities, insurance, rent, and contributions to retirement accounts and compare the cost of each to their cost in previous years. The fixed expenses may have increased. A business owner is powerless when it comes to electricity rates or the cost of heating fuel. He or she should also consider any unexpected, one-time cash outlays that have affected the bottom line. One of the stores may have needed a new heating system or a new roof. Perhaps the stores needed to build ramps to comply with the Americans with Disabilities Act. Without a comprehensive financial picture, the owner may make changes that could lead to further financial decline for Movies Galore.

The owner assumes that Movies Galore's low prices are a big draw for the business. That may be true, but it is just as likely that the convenient hours of operation make his business popular. It should be simple to determine which hours of operation are the busiest in each location. The downtown location in Marston may thrive by closing at six, but mall or suburban locations may benefit from staying open later. Keeping low prices and cutting back hours may be counterproductive. How do his prices compare with those of his competitors? He may be able to raise his prices and keep them lower than theirs. Without operating hours that are convenient for each location, this business may see a decline in patronage. In some cases, he may be able to open later rather than close earlier. In addition, the owner has changed the stores' inventory by eliminating DVDs that were released more than five years ago. Chances are that those older DVDs cost less to purchase than new releases, enabling the owner to charge less for them. In some of the chain's locations, older movies may be very popular, and, by eliminating them, the stores could lose customers.

There are several reasons for the owner of Movies Galore to re-evaluate his decision to limit stocked films and store hours. While a change in the company's business model may be needed, this change should reflect the needs and desires of the local customers. By disregarding these needs, the owner risks sending his company into further financial ruin.

Argument Task 19

The following appeared in a letter to the editor of a local newspaper

"Commuters complain that increased rush-hour traffic on Blue Highway between the suburbs and the city center has doubled their commuting time. The favored proposal of the motorists' lobby is to widen the highway, adding an additional lane of traffic. But last year's addition of a lane to the nearby Green Highway was followed by a worsening of traffic jams on it. A better alternative is to add a bicycle lane to Blue Highway. Many area residents are keen bicyclists. A bicycle lane would encourage them to use bicycles to commute, and so would reduce rush-hour traffic rather than fostering an increase."

Write a response in which you discuss what specific evidence is needed to evaluate the argument and explain how the evidence would weaken or strengthen the argument.

Strategies

Argument:

Based on the results of adding an additional lane to the Green Highway, the writer argues that adding a bike lane to the Blue Highway is a better alternative to an additional traffic lane.

Claims and Assumptions:

a) The writer claims that commuting time between the suburbs and the city have doubled on the Blue Highway. The assumption is that the highway does not have sufficient lanes to handle the volume of traffic. Another assumption might be that more vehicles than before are traveling on this road during rush hours. The reader needs to know why there is an apparent increase in traffic. Has there been an interruption in public transportation? Are fewer commuters carpooling? Did a Park and Ride close? Is all of the rush-hour traffic attributed to people going to and from work? Has an attempt been made to actually count the cars?

b) The writer also claims that, since the addition of a lane on the Green Highway, there have been worsening traffic jams. The assumption here is that an additional lane may have been the cause of the traffic jams. One is left to wonder why there appears to be increased traffic difficulties on both highways. Do traffic jams continue to be a problem on Green Highway?

c) Many area residents are bicycle enthusiasts. The writer assumes that, if there were a bike lane, many of those cyclists would ride their bikes to work. Can commuters travel in this manner year-round? Will they bike to work in the rain? What about when the days are shorter and they must travel in the dark? Are there enough places to store or park bikes safely during the work day? Which area residents are keen bicyclists?

Your notes do not have to be exhaustive. As you begin to write your essay, your brain will generate new ideas. Make certain that you keep the directions in mind as you develop your ideas.

Sample Essay

The writer of this editorial is expressing his opinion about a way to relieve apparent traffic jams on Blue Highway. Either the writer or people he has spoken to complain that commuting time between the suburbs and the city center has doubled. The motorists' lobby proposes adding a lane to the highway, but the writer, citing trouble on Green Highway since it added a lane for cars, suggests that a bike lane would be a better solution to the problem on Blue Highway. Decision makers need more evidence about the traffic situation on both highways before opting for either choice.

The reader assumes that a doubling of commuting time must mean a doubling of the number of cars traveling on Blue Highway. An increase in the number of vehicles may be partially responsible, but it could be that the highway department reduced the speed on the highway as well. Where have the extra vehicles come from? The decision makers may discover that another traffic artery is partially or completed closed for construction, and the increased traffic may be temporary.

Comparing Blue Highway's problems to those of Green Highway in unproductive. The two roads carry traffic from different areas and, maybe, for different purposes. To support the addition of a bike lane, the writer must present evidence that bike lanes effectively reduce automobile traffic in cities where there is a large volume of commuters. That should be a simple matter of contacting other urban areas that have bike lanes used by commuters.

For commuters to agree that biking is a suitable alternative to driving to work, they will need evidence of security for their bikes in the city. Are there now or will there be in the future facilities where bicyclists can safely park their bikes during the work day. They also might need some incentive to ride bikes rather than drive cars to work each day. What have other cities done if anything? After all, these cyclists are helping to reduce pollution and rush-hour traffic jams. Shouldn't there be some reward? Has the author surveyed cyclists to determine their number and their willingness to commute by bike? Has he checked a meteorological survey to discover how many days a year, on average, are suitable for traveling by bike?

Can this writer provide evidence that the city can save construction costs by adding bike lanes rather than another lane for vehicles? One might imagine that the specifications for a bike lane would be less onerous than that for a lane of traffic expected to carry thousands of passenger cars and heavy commercial vehicles. Because bikes travel in the same direction as motorized vehicles, the city would need to build a lane on each side of the highway. Is there room on both sides of the highway for a bike lane?

In a culture that has a continuing love affair with the automobile, the author will need a raft of evidence to support the building of bike lanes rather than an additional lane for cars and trucks. He also needs evidence to show how an additional lane for vehicles is not the answer to alleviating the commuter dilemmas on Blue Highway.

Argument Task 20

> *The following appeared in a memo from the vice president of a food distribution company with food storage warehouses in several cities.*
>
> *"Recently, we signed a contract with the Fly-Away Pest Control Company to provide pest control services at our fast-food warehouse in Palm City, but last month we discovered that over $20,000 worth of food there had been destroyed by pest damage. Meanwhile, the Buzzoff Pest Control Company, which we have used for many years, continued to service our warehouse in Wintervale, and last month only $10,000 worth of the food stored there had been destroyed by pest damage. Even though the price charged by Fly-Away is considerably lower, our best means of saving money is to return to Buzzoff for all our pest control services."*
>
> Write a response in which you discuss what specific evidence is needed to evaluate the argument and explain how the evidence would weaken or strengthen the argument.

Strategies

A good place to start your analysis is by creating a statement that reveals the main idea of the argument. Although the writer is creating an argument, he may ultimately be stating a position, making a recommendation, or making a prediction. It may be helpful for you to determine which of these formats is most evident in the argument.

As a result of food spoilage in the Palm City warehouse, the vice president of the company recommends a return to using Buzzoff pest control services.

Assumptions:

a) Conditions at both warehouses are identical.

b) The same type of pest is present at both warehouses.

c) The food stored in both warehouses is equally attractive to pests.

d) Both warehouses are the same size and require the same amount of pest-control product.

e) The higher cost of Buzzoff services will be offset by a reduction in food spoilage.

f) The amount of the loss is greater than in previous years.

Evidence needed to evaluate the argument:

a) The types of food stored at each facility

b) The types of pests present at each facility

c) Other conditions that may have resulted in spoilage

d) Why the company decided to use a different company for its facility in Palm City

e) How much food is stored at each warehouse?

    f)   The percentage of the food that was spoiled at each warehouse

After completing these steps, you should have enough material to write your analysis. Remember that you are not creating a position of your own; you are evaluating the strengths and weaknesses of the existing argument. You do not have to include all of the points that you have created in your prewriting. In fact, during the process of drafting your analysis, other ideas may come to mind, and, if they strengthen your analysis, you should include them.

Sample Essay

Food is perishable. It must be stored at correct temperatures and humidity. Even when those conditions are managed correctly, pests are still a threat. Some may arrive with the food from its country of origin, while others invade at its arrival point. This company has hired two companies to control the pests at its warehouses, and, according to the manager, one has been more successful than the other. Before the owners of the company take the suggestion to return all of the pest control to Buzzoff, they need more evidence of Fly Away's inability to keep their products free from pests.

First, the owners should know what prompted the switch to Fly Away. There might be evidence that Buzzoff had not been as successful in Palm City as they had been in previous years or in the company's other locations. Buzzoff may have been too busy to continue servicing the Palm City warehouse and may not even be able to do so if asked in the future. On the other hand, Fly Away may have approached the food company and made promises that they could not keep. If that is the case, the company is justified in returning to Buzzoff.

Some foods are more susceptible to invasions of pests. The strength of the recommendation may rest on knowing the types of food at each location. Palm City stores fast food, but the argument does not reveal what type of fast food. In fact, if this warehouse provides storage for ground beef, temperature, rather than pests would be the likely culprit for spoilage. Fly Away may have been effective in eliminating pests, but a refrigeration problem would cause the bacteria already present in ground meat to cause its breakdown. The warehouse in Palm City may have some structural damage that could allow pests like rats or raccoons to get into the building and feast on the product within. Fly Away may not have been instructed to poison or trap these critters. The warehouse in Wintervale may store frozen food exclusively, so pests are not a big problem. The $10,000 loss could have resulted from a malfunction in a unit or even an issue with a delivery truck. On the other hand, both warehouses may be perfectly maintained, store the same type of food, and Fly Away did an inferior job at pest control in Palm City. It would be important to know how much food is stored at each warehouse. The argument provides the dollar amount of loss at each location, but not the percentage of total inventory lost to pests. It appears that the $10,000 loss in Wintervale is not as alarming as the $20,000 loss in Palm City. If, however, the Palm City warehouse stores $200,000 worth of product, and the Wintervale warehouse stores $100,000 worth of product, the percentage of loss is the same. Companies that deal with perishable merchandise usually have some level of acceptable loss, but that information is not present in the argument. In fact, they may have had bigger losses last year. This year's loss to pests might be average.

Environmental anomalies could account for Fly Away's apparent failure to protect the food stored in the Palm City warehouse. Temperatures may have been much higher or lower than usual. There may have been significantly more rain or humidity. Some insect populations are cyclical. Fly Away may have contracted to do the job for a specific price that was suitable for average conditions. If the conditions were extraordinary in some way, any company would have found it difficult or impossible to prevent the loss. Additionally, conditions in Wintervale may have been more favorable than normal, helping to make the loss there significantly smaller.

The loss of product in either or both warehouses may have been beyond the company's control regardless of which pest service it used. The pest problem may have originated with the company's suppliers. The vice president doesn't reveal if he or one of his managers decided to buy product from a new supplier. If the loss to pests this year is unacceptable, the company needs clearer evidence that Fly Away rather than some other contingency is the cause. It may turn out that Fly Away is an excellent choice for pest control, and the easiest way to save money is to use them for all the company's warehouses.

Argument Task 21

> *The following appeared as a recommendation by a committee planning a ten-year budget for the city of Calatrava.*
>
> *"The birthrate in our city is declining: in fact, last year's birthrate was only one-half that of five years ago. Thus the number of students enrolled in our public schools will soon decrease dramatically, and we can safely reduce the funds budgeted for education during the next decade. At the same time, we can reduce funding for athletic playing fields and other recreational facilities. As a result, we will have sufficient money to fund city facilities and programs used primarily by adults, since we can expect the adult population of the city to increase."*
>
> Write a response in which you discuss what specific evidence is needed to evaluate the argument and explain how the evidence would weaken or strengthen the argument.

Strategies

Argument:

Because of declining birthrates, the city can redirect funds it has habitually spent on facilities for young people to programs for adults.

In developing your response, you must determine what evidence the planning committee needs to uncover before making its final budget decisions for the next ten-year cycle.

Facts and Assumptions:

a) Last year's birthrate was half of that five years ago. The assumption is that the birth rate has been declining steadily. Is last year's birthrate an anomaly? What was the birthrate in the intervening years? How many births were there 5 years ago? If there were only 4 births, for example, then half of that is not a huge drop. If there were 100 births 5 years ago, then half of that is cause for concern.

b) The committee assumes that the lower birth rate predicts a smaller school population. The committee reasons that the school budget can, therefore, be reduced. Does the committee have any figures on the number of families that may have moved to the town?

c) The committee uses its assumption of a smaller school population to suggest that less money be spent on athletic playing fields and other recreational facilities. Even if the number of young people declines, won't those remaining still play sports and use the recreational facilities? Might residents be willing to pay to use the facilities to offset the cost of maintaining them? Are the facilities used only by children?

d) The committee suggests diverting funds previously used on youth facilities to fund facilities and programs used primarily by adults. The assumption is that the adult population will increase as the youth population decreases. If there is a decline in the birth rate, won't there be a corresponding decline in the number of people who become adults? Have other towns had success doing this? How does the town attract new residents if it has let its facilities for young people decline in quality?

Your notes do not have to be exhaustive. As you begin to write your essay, your brain will generate new ideas. Make certain that you keep the directions in mind as you develop your ideas.

Sample Essay

Unless one is planning a retirement community, catering to the needs of adults at the expense of the children is an unwise choice. It is sometimes easy to relegate children to the background when making budgetary decisions. Children don't vote or pay taxes. When there is an apparent decline in the number of children requiring services traditionally reserved for them in a town, it becomes easier to divert funds for their benefit to programs and facilities that focus on adults. Those voters and taxpayers whose own children have grown are now focused on their own needs and may see decisions that benefit them as the correct ones. City stakeholders must take a closer look at the facts presented by the planning committee before making any long-term decisions for the community.

The apparently drastic decline in the birthrate seems to justify the committee's recommendation. When citizens are told that the birthrate last year was just half of what is was five years ago, visions of empty classrooms and playing fields fill their heads. It would be logical to assume that fewer tax dollars will be needed to educate and entertain the young people of Calatrava. What these residents must do first is to more closely examine this statistic. How many children were born in Calatrava five years ago, and how many were born last year? A decline of fifty percent is alarming. However, if there were only four births in Calatrava five years ago, then last year's births totaled two. Two fewer births is hardly a cause to fire teachers, close schools, or let playing fields become decrepit. Upon further investigation, the committee may discover that, five years ago, Calatrava recorded fifty births and last year only twenty-five births. Twenty-five children represent an average classroom population. That figure might justify eliminating an elementary school teaching position. The committee should also look at the intervening years. Is last year's birth rate a fluke? Was the birthrate of five years ago repeated or, even, surpassed in the years that followed? In addition to births, the population of children is affected by families moving in and out of Calatrava. The planning committee can access information about home sales and how many families have moved into or out of the city to get an accurate picture of the city's demographics.

Forestalling maintenance of athletic fields and recreational facilities may seem like a prudent move if, indeed, the population of children has declined significantly. The fact remains that the children of the town will still participate in school athletics and recreational activities. If the fields and facilities deteriorate, other towns may be reluctant to bring their teams to Calatrava to compete. Calatrava teams will have to travel more frequently to complete their athletic schedules, and this would be an expense that might offset the savings gained by ignoring the fields at home. Do adults in the community use these facilities? Does the town have an adult softball league that plays its games on the school athletic fields? Do adults as well as children use the community swimming pool?

Calatrava's planning committee must dig more deeply into the facts that they have used to make their preliminary recommendations. The taxpayers should demand to know that their tax dollars are being spent in a way that benefits the greatest number of residents.

Argument Task 22

> *The following appeared in a letter to the editor of Parson City's local newspaper.*
>
> *"In our region of Trillura, the majority of money spent on the schools that most students attend - the city-run public schools - comes from taxes that each city government collects. The region's cities differ, however, in the budgetary priority they give to public education. For example, both as a proportion of its overall tax revenues and in absolute terms, Parson City has recently spent almost twice as much per year as Blue City has for its public schools—even though both cities have about the same number of residents. Clearly, Parson City residents place a higher value on providing a good education in public schools than Blue City residents do."*
>
> Write a response in which you discuss what specific evidence is needed to evaluate the argument and explain how the evidence would weaken or strengthen the argument.

Strategies

Argument:

Because Parson City has spent twice as much of its tax revenue as Blue City has on education, Parson City places a greater value on providing a good education as does Blue City.

In developing your response, you must determine what evidence the planning committee needs to uncover before making its final budget decisions for its City spends on its public school students demonstrates that it place more value on education than Blue City does.

Facts and Assumptions:

a)   The majority of money spent on public schools in Trillura comes from city tax revenue.

b)   Parson City has recently spent almost twice as much per year as Blue City has for its public schools. The logical assumption that follows is that Parson City spends twice as much per student as Blue City does. Blue City may have more students on private schools. Parson City may have recently had to replace one of its schools, adding a significant amount to its yearly school budget. The word recently is a qualifier. Did Blue City spend more than Parson City in the past?

c)   Parson City and Blue City have about the same number of residents. This may lead to the assumption that each city has the same number of public school students. In fact, Blue City may have a very different demographic than Parson City.

Your notes do not have to be exhaustive. As you begin to write your essay, your brain will generate new ideas. Make certain that you keep the directions in mind as you develop your ideas.

Sample Essay

In this letter to the editor, the writer has taken the position that Parson City places a higher value on educating its children than does Blue City. The writer cites budget figures from the two cities to support his position. Since letters to the editor express an opinion, the reader should always accept the facts with a good deal of skepticism. Acknowledging that the writer's purpose is to persuade, the reader should demand some concrete evidence before accepting that opinion as fact.

The author's first statement is likely true. It is the case in most communities everywhere that local schools are supported, in large part, by local tax dollars and that the largest part of a community's budget is expended on its schools. However, to suggest that the amount of money that a community spends is a reflection of the value it places on education is misleading. A number of factors influence how much of a city's budget, both in real dollars and percentage of the total budget, is allocated for public schools. The reader should seek evidence of the existence of any extenuating circumstances that would account for the greater amount spent in Parson City.

Consider the demographic of each community. The author states that both communities have about the same number of residents, a statement easily verified by looking at census results. The composition of each city's total may vary. Again, by scrutinizing census records, one can discover how many residents comprise each age group. If Parson City has considerably more school-age children than Blue City does, the reason for the greater expenditure on public schools becomes patently obvious. Blue City, in fact, may be home to an aging population. A large portion of that city's budget may go to services for the elderly.

In addition, Parson City may have had to replace an aging school building, leaking roofs or windows, or an antiquated heating system. Any of those capital improvements would influence the school budget for a few years. The writer uses the word recently when comparing the two communities' public school expenditures. Is there evidence that, at some period in the recent past, Blue City spent more than Parson City on its schools? Blue City may have recently finished paying for capital improvements to its schools and, as a result, has been able to reduce its school budget.

A final assumption is that spending more money on education makes that education better. More money can buy more books and the latest technology; it can build beautiful schools and reduce classroom size. However, only the school district's philosophy can create good education. Many schools deliver an excellent education to its students while operating on a shoestring. Good education is measured by the achievement of students, not by the size of the budget.

In its current form, this letter to the editor provides too many vague statements and too little evidence for the reader to accept that Parson City places more value on education than does Blue City. Only if facts are uncovered to support the idea that Parson City is spending more per pupil than Blue City is can the residents of Parson City feel a sense of superiority regarding education in its public schools.

Argument Task 23

The following appeared in a memo from a vice president of Quiot Manufacturing.

"During the past year, Quiot Manufacturing had 30 percent more on-the-job accidents than at the nearby Panoply Industries plant, where the work shifts are one hour shorter than ours. Experts say that significant contributing factors in many on-the-job accidents are fatigue and sleep deprivation among workers. Therefore, to reduce the number of on-the-job accidents at Quiot and thereby increase productivity, we should shorten each of our three work shifts by one hour so that employees will get adequate amounts of sleep."

Write a response in which you examine the stated and/or unstated assumptions of the argument. Be sure to explain how the argument depends on these assumptions and what the implications are for the argument if the assumptions prove unwarranted.

Strategies

Argument:

Shortening each shift at Quiot Manufacturing will reduce the number of workplace accidents.

Assumptions:

a) The workers at Quiot Manufacturing are fatigued. Are the employees found sleeping on the job?

b) The workers at Quiot Manufacturing suffer from sleep deprivation. Have studies been done to confirm this?

c) Fatigue and/or sleep deprivation are the cause of on-the- job accidents at Quiot Manufacturing. Is the work environment safe? Do employees follow appropriate safety measures?

d) Panoply Industries has fewer accidents because their workers are better rested. Do workers there perform the same kind of tasks as the workers at Quiot?

e) If work shifts are shortened, workers will get more sleep. Workers are just as likely to use the extra time to go shopping, socialize, or watch television.

Your notes do not have to be exhaustive. As you begin to write your essay, your brain will generate new ideas. Make certain that you keep the directions in mind as you develop your ideas.

Sample Essay

Quiot Manufacturing's vice president has used faulty reasoning to reach the conclusion that shortening work shifts will reduce the number of on-the-job accidents at the plant. Fatigue and sleep deprivation certainly can contribute to workplace accidents, but so can several other factors. Before deciding to shorten the work shifts, the managers should consider all the conditions that affect safety at Quiot Manufacturing.

The vice president of the company assumes that worker fatigue is the culprit behind the high number of on-the-job accidents. Is there evidence of fatigue? Are workers falling asleep on the job? Are they coming to work late? Has anyone surveyed the employees? Without answers to these questions, his assumption may be erroneous. He may be basing his assumption on the fact that Panoply Industries, with its shorter work shifts, has fewer workplace accidents. The writer should examine the reasons behind Panoply's lower incidence of accidents at its facility.

If it turns out to be true that the workers at Quiot Manufacturing are sleep deprived, what is the cause? Most workdays are eight hours, and that is likely the length of each shift at the company. If Quiot workers are not spending more time than the average worker on the job, the length of the work day is not the most logical cause of their fatigue. The nature of the work may be tiring. Is it arduous, physically taxing, or is it monotonous and boring? Regularly scheduled breaks may solve that.

Quiot Manufacturing should examine its own culpability for creating an unsafe workplace. Has the company installed safety equipment that reduces accidents? Have the workers been trained to follow appropriate safety procedures? If the managers at Quiot were to question Panoply Industries, they may find that Panoply has recently reduced the number of accidents occurring at its plant. They may have installed safety features and instituted employee training that account for the lower incidence of accidents. On the other hand, safety features and training may be identical at both businesses and the shorter shifts have led to a reduction in accidents.

This writer must discover the actual figures behind the 30 percent more accidents at Quiot Manufacturing. How many accidents did each company report? If Panoply reported 3 on-the-job accidents, and Quiot had 30 percent more than that, then Quiot reported 4 accidents. This is hardly a number worth changing the structure of work shifts at the plant. On the other hand, if Panoply Industries reported 30 accidents, then Quiot Manufacturing would have had 39 accidents. An additional 9 accidents would be cause for concern, and the company should investigate the cause.

Shorter shifts may not improve either workplace safety or productivity. The vice president assumes that workers will rest more if they work less. The workers are just as likely to use the extra time to go shopping, socialize with friends, or watch television. Introspection may be a better approach than innovation to ensure worker safety and increased productivity.

Argument Task 24

> *The following report appeared in the newsletter of the West Meria Public Health Council.*
>
> *"An innovative treatment has come to our attention that promises to significantly reduce absenteeism in our schools and workplaces. A study reports that in nearby East Meria, where fish consumption is very high, people visit the doctor only once or twice per year for the treatment of colds. Clearly, eating a substantial amount of fish can prevent colds. Since colds represent the most frequently given reason for absences from school and work, we recommend the daily use of Ichthaid - a nutritional supplement derived from fish oil - as a good way to prevent colds and lower absenteeism."*
>
> Write a response in which you discuss what specific evidence is needed to evaluate the argument and explain how the evidence would weaken or strengthen the argument.

NOTE: *The above topic has wording similar to Argument Task 15 of GRE Analytical Writing Solution to the Real Essay Topics - Book 2. However, if you read carefully you will notice that the task instructions are different. Hence, it is very important to read the topic as well as its instructions completely before you start to write your response.*

Strategies

Argument:

The daily use of Ichthaid will prevent colds and lower absenteeism.

In developing your response, you must demonstrate what evidence is needed to support the recommendation that citizens of West Meria take the supplement, Ichthaid.

Facts and Assumptions:

a) People in East Meria visit the doctor only once or twice per year for the treatment of colds. The writer assumes that this number is lower than elsewhere. The reader may wonder if the residents have colds that they don't seek treatment for.

b) Fish consumption is high in East Meria. The writer has made a connection between high fish consumption and a presumed low incidence of colds. Are the residents taking some other preventive measure to reduce the number of colds? Are they eating a diet rich in vitamin C or taking Echinacea supplements? They may be eating fish with lots of lemon, a fruit high in vitamin C. Does everyone eat fish? Do colds afflict non-fish eaters more than those who do eat fish?

c) Colds represent the most frequently given reason for absences from school and work. The writer assumes that the workers and students have reported truthfully. Because colds are so common, they make a convenient excuse. The writer assumes that reducing the number of colds that people get, the less absenteeism there will be.

d) Ichthaid is a nutritional supplement derived from fish oil. The writer assumes that this supplement will have the same supposed healthful effect as eating fish. Can the community force its residents to take this supplement? Will the cost of the supplement prevent some from taking it?

Your notes do not have to be exhaustive. As you begin to write your essay, your brain will generate new ideas. Make certain that you keep the directions in mind as you develop your ideas.

Sample Essay

The author of this newsletter has combined two ostensibly unrelated facts to form a conclusion that is not supported by evidence. In addition, the writer has made a sweeping recommendation based on the original faulty assumptions. The residents of West Meria should scrutinize these statements before accepting the writer's recommendation to take the dietary supplement, Ichthaid.

According to the newsletter, the citizens of East Meria both eat a lot of fish and make few visits to the doctor for the treatment of colds. The writer assumes that this is an example of cause-and-effect. What evidence exists to support this? First, the reader should ask to know if East Meria's residents visit a doctor for treatment of every cold. It is likely that many people treat their colds themselves; after all, there is no cure. Next, they should ask how many of those cold sufferers are habitual fish eaters.

If East Merians do, in fact, contract fewer colds than average, they may be taking other preventive measures. Is there evidence that they take vitamin C or Echinacea? They may be eating large quantities of fresh fruits and vegetables, most of which are rich in vitamin C and other nutrients that contribute to good health. They may even be eating their fish with lots of lemon, a fruit known to be high in vitamin C.

The writer is probably accurate when he informs the reader that colds are the most often used excuse for absence from school and work. Since the cold is so common, it is a convenient excuse for anyone needing a day off from work or school. However, it is also common for students to avoid attending class by falsely claiming to be sick. How many students actually have colds? Even if colds can be prevented by taking the supplement, Ichthaid, can the same be said for absenteeism?

Nutritional supplements are popular and a seemingly harmless way to remedy deficits in one's diet. The citizens of West Meria should probably look for evidence of studies done on Ichthaid before accepting the recommendation in this newsletter. Supplements are neither always harmless nor effective. The expense and possible negative side effects should make them think twice, or, to paraphrase Marie Antoinette, "Let them eat fish."

Argument Task 25

The following appeared in a recommendation from the planning department of the city of Transopolis.

"Ten years ago, as part of a comprehensive urban renewal program, the city of Transopolis adapted for industrial use a large area of severely substandard housing near the freeway. Subsequently, several factories were constructed there, crime rates in the area declined, and property tax revenues for the entire city increased. To further revitalize the city, we should now take similar action in a declining residential area on the opposite side of the city. Since some houses and apartments in existing nearby neighborhoods are currently unoccupied, alternate housing for those displaced by this action will be readily available."

Write a response in which you discuss what specific evidence is needed to evaluate the argument and explain how the evidence would weaken or strengthen the argument.

Strategies

Argument:

To further revitalize Transopolis, the city should extend its urban renewal program to another declining residential area of the city.

In developing your response, you are asked to identify evidence that Transopolis needs to carry out its urban renewal plan.

Facts and Assumptions:

a) Since Transopolis replaced substandard housing with an industrial complex, crime rates in the area have declined. The writer assumes that one action has led to the other. It is just as likely that an area with fewer people will have less crime. Has crime increased in other parts of the city?

b) Tax revenues have increased for the entire city. Did the city have to expend any of its revenues to either buy out or relocate the former residents of the substandard housing? The new tax revenues may limply offset previous expenses. Will the city have to use its funds to develop the new proposed location?

c) There is demand for more development in Transopolis. This assumption underlies the recommendation to remove a neighborhood in decline and repeat the development already completed on the other side of town.

d) Some housing is available close to the proposed development for residents who will be displaced.

e) The assumption that it makes more economic sense to relocate people to empty houses and apartments rather than locate the development there and leave the residents where they are.

Your notes do not have to be exhaustive. As you begin to write your essay, your brain will generate new ideas. Make certain that you keep the directions in mind as you develop your ideas.

Sample Essay

Before moving forward with plans to develop an additional part of the city, planners should consider the real benefits of doing so. They should look for evidence to support the claims of reduced crime and increased tax revenues along with evidence of a need for more development. The current owners of the land and buildings or the contractors who complete the work may be the only beneficiaries.

The planning committee reports a reduction in crime because of the previous urban renewal project. That might be expected in an area that is now devoted to factories. The committee needs evidence that crime has not simply been moved to another part of the city along with the residents. Simply displacing crime is not a justification for further development. Is there evidence of significant crime in the location proposed for the new development? If not, that rationale won't fly. Moving crime to a different part of the city does not makes residents safer or save the city any money.

The planners may be living with a field of Dreams mentality: if we build it, they will come. Does the city have manufacturers clamoring for space in Transopolis? If the city buys out the residents of the area and erects buildings on speculation, it may find itself a landlord of empty buildings with a sizable budget deficit. The taxpayers should demand to know that there is a guaranteed return on their investment. Otherwise, this development could wipe out any extra revenues from the previous urban renewal. Evidence is needed to support the choice of location for the new revitalization effort. The planner proposes moving residents of the declining neighborhood to nearby neighborhoods where some houses and apartments are unoccupied. Further research may demonstrate that it would be more fiscally and humanely sound to place the new development where residences are already unoccupied. There is too little evidence in this passage to show that one location has advantages over the other.

The city needs evidence of easy access to the proposed location. The original site is near the freeway, providing a means for workers and commercial vehicles to get there. Located on the opposite side of the city, the proposed site may require building new or widening existing roads. The result could be additional displacement of Transopolis citizens and/ or a reduction in property values.

All stakeholders of the city should complete more investigation of this proposal of the planning department before giving a green signal. It would be easy to get on board with the planning department considering the previous successes. However, Transopolis may have completed all the development that it can presently handle or needs.

Argument Task 26

> *The following appeared in a memo from the new vice president of Sartorian, a company that manufactures men's clothing.*
>
> *"Five years ago, at a time when we had difficulties in obtaining reliable supplies of high quality wool fabric, we discontinued production of our alpaca overcoat. Now that we have a new fabric supplier, we should resume production. This coat should sell very well: since we have not offered an alpaca overcoat for five years and since our major competitor no longer makes an alpaca overcoat, there will be pent-up customer demand. Also, since the price of most types of clothing has increased in each of the past five years, customers should be willing to pay significantly higher prices for alpaca overcoats than they did five years ago, and our company profits will increase."*
>
> Write a response in which you discuss what specific evidence is needed to evaluate the argument and explain how the evidence would weaken or strengthen the argument.

Strategies

Argument:

Based on the ability to obtain high quality fabric and an opportunity to corner the market, Sartorian will reintroduce its alpaca overcoat.

In developing your response, reveal the specific evidence that Sartorian needs to decide whether or not reintroducing its alpaca coat is a sound idea.

Facts and Assumptions:

a) Five years ago, Sartorian discontinued production of its alpaca overcoat because it lacked a reliable supply of high quality wool fabric. There must be very few suppliers of alpaca wool fabric.

b) Sartorian has a new supplier of fabric. A new producer has come about or the quality of a previous supplier has improved enough to satisfy Sartorian.

c) Sartorian has not offered an alpaca coat for five years. The company assumes that it customers are eager for the company's new coat.

d) Sartorian's major competitor no longer makes an alpaca coat. Sartorian may assume that the competitor's coat did not measure up, and customers stopped buying it. Sartorian needs to consider that the competitor's coat may have been lovely, but demand for alpaca coats or the cost of production made it unwise to continue producing them.

e) The price of most types of clothing has increased in each of the past five years. The assumption is that customers have become used to higher prices and will be agreeable to higher prices for the alpaca coat. Sartorian believes that higher prices for its coat will increase company profits.

Your notes do not have to be exhaustive. As you begin to write your essay, your brain will generate new ideas. Make certain that you keep the directions in mind as you develop your ideas.

Sample Essay

Sartorian appears eager to jump back into the alpaca coat market after a five-year absence. The company must have a strong emotional attachment to the coat they used to make and sell with some success. One is left to wonder if discontinuing the coat left a gap in their clothing line that it has been unable to fill with another garment. The lack of competition in the alpaca coat market seems a further incentive to resume production. Sartorian has drawn some conclusions that bear further scrutiny before taking what is probably an expensive step.

The clothing manufacturer assumes that its customer loyalty guarantees the success of its alpaca coat. The stores who formerly sold the coat may have replaced it with other outer garments with which they are very satisfied. As a result, those stores may not have the money to stock the new alpaca coats. Sartorian should survey the buyers for retail outlets that sold their previous coat as well as any new stores. The manufacturer may discover that it cannot generate sales sufficient to justify reintroducing the alpaca coat.

Sartorian seems encouraged by the lack of competition in the alpaca coat market. Its only competitor has ceased production of its own coat. Sartorian would be well-advised to interview the other manufacturer to uncover the reason for stopping production. The truth of the matter may be that alpaca coats have fallen completely out of favor. The pent-up customer demand that Sartorian is anticipating may not exist.

The final justification that Sartorian cites is the overall increase in clothing prices over the past five years. The company assumes that they will be able to demand higher prices for its alpaca coat, which will help the company's bottom line. The truth may be that individual clothing budgets may be strained by the rise in prices, and there is no money left over with which to buy an expensive alpaca coat.

Sartorian's vice president has some research to do before jumping back into the alpaca coat market. He needs evidence of continuing demand for the product. Cornering the market for a clothing item that won't sell would not be a feather in this vice president's hat.

Argument Task 27

> A recent sales study indicates that consumption of seafood dishes in Bay City restaurants has increased by 30 percent during the past five years. Yet there are no currently operating city restaurants whose specialty is seafood. Moreover, the majority of families in Bay City are two-income families, and a nationwide study has shown that such families eat significantly fewer home-cooked meals than they did a decade ago but at the same time express more concern about healthful eating. Therefore, the new Captain Seafood restaurant that specializes in seafood should be quite popular and profitable.
>
> Write a response in which you discuss what specific evidence is needed to evaluate the argument and explain how the evidence would weaken or strengthen the argument.

NOTE: *The above topic has wording similar to Argument Task 17 of GRE Analytical Writing Solution to the Real Essay Topics - Book 2. However, if you read carefully you will notice that the task instructions are different. Hence, it is very important to read the topic as well as its instructions completely before you start to write your response.*

Strategies

Argument:

Based on the apparent popularity of seafood dishes, the new Captain Seafood restaurant should be popular and profitable in Bay City.

In developing your response, you must identify what evidence is needed to show that the new restaurant will indeed be both popular and profitable.

Facts and Assumptions:

a) The consumption of seafood dishes in Bay City restaurants has increased by 30 percent during the past five years. The assumption is that the consumption of seafood dishes is very high. The truth of that depends on the level of consumption five years ago. Sales of these dishes have increased by roughly one-third, so any restaurant that used to sell 3 seafood dishes each day is now selling 4.

b) There are currently no operating restaurants that specialize in seafood. Were there seafood restaurants in the past? What happened to them?

c) Bay City has a large number of two-income families, and studies show that this type of family eats significantly fewer home-cooked meals than they did a decade ago. The assumption is that these families eat out frequently. They are just as likely to buy prepared food at the grocery store. What does significantly mean? Again, the reader needs to know the level of home-cooked meals that these families ate a decade ago.

d) These same families express more concern about healthful eating. One assumption implied by this statement is that those families actually are eating more healthy meals. Another assumption is that the seafood dishes being served in restaurants are healthy.

Your notes do not have to be exhaustive. As you begin to write your essay, your brain will generate new ideas. Make certain that you keep the directions in mind as you develop your ideas.

Sample Essay

The writer offers the reader some statistics that presume to prove a significant increase in the popularity of seafood dishes in Bay City's restaurants even though none of those eateries specialize in seafood. Some might mistakenly understand that seafood entrees comprise 30 percent of restaurant sales, and that would be impressive. In actuality, the sale of such dishes has increased by 30 percent, or roughly 1/3, over the past five years. If we know that restaurant A sold 6 seafood dishes each day five years ago, then we can calculate that the same restaurant sells 8 per day now. An increase of two dishes per day is not cause for celebration. Should we discover, however, that restaurant A sold 30 seafood dishes every day five years ago, a 30 percent increase would now be 40 dishes per day. Depending on the restaurant's overall volume, an additional 10 seafood dishes might be meaningful.

Another statistic employed by the writer relates to the domestic habits of the two-income families that comprise most of Bay City's population. Nationwide studies show that families in this demographic eat significantly fewer home-cooked meals than they did a decade ago. Significant is a subjective term. What is significant for one family may be trifling for another. The reader would be wise to apply the logic from the previous paragraph to this fact. In addition, the fact that they eat fewer home-cooked meals does not lead inevitably to the conclusion that they are not eating at home. These families may very well be purchasing prepared or frozen meals at the local supermarket. Counting on their patronage to ensure the popularity and profitability of a new restaurant would be a mistake without further evidence about their dining habits.

The same study cited in the previous paragraph reveals that two-income families express more concern about healthy eating. Expressing concern and taking some action are two widely different concepts. Many people are concerned about heart disease but continue to smoke. In the context of this passage, the writer would lead the reader to assume that seafood entrees are more healthful than other dishes. A fillet of haddock smothered in buttered bread crumbs or served with a cream sauce is no healthier for a dinner than a lean piece of beef cooked on the grill. The writer should examine the menus at the restaurants to determine the ingredients and cooking methods used for the seafood dishes. If the entrees are baked, steamed, or poached and served with lemon and fresh vegetables, they could be considered more healthful than dishes that naturally have more animal fat and cholesterol.

Finally, the writer claims that the current lack of a restaurant specializing in seafood in Bay City is certain to ensure the success of the new Captain Seafood restaurant. Was there a seafood restaurant in Bay City at one time? If so, why did it close? If a seafood restaurant closed in the city, which could account, at least in part, for the increase in seafood entrees' popularity in the other eateries. A closer examination of some of the facts and assumptions in the passage reveals that the popularity and profitability of Captain Seafood is not a foregone conclusion. It relies on evidence that easily could be obtained to support the writer's claim.

Argument Task 28

> Milk and dairy products are rich in vitamin D and calcium - substances essential for building and maintaining bones. Many people therefore say that a diet rich in dairy products can help prevent osteoporosis, a disease that is linked to both environmental and genetic factors and that causes the bones to weaken significantly with age. But a long-term study of a large number of people found that those who consistently consumed dairy products throughout the years of the study have a higher rate of bone fractures than any other participants in the study. Since bone fractures are symptomatic of osteoporosis, this study result shows that a diet rich in dairy products may actually increase, rather than decrease, the risk of osteoporosis.
>
> Write a response in which you discuss what specific evidence is needed to evaluate the argument and explain how the evidence would weaken or strengthen the argument.

Strategies

Argument:

The results of a long-term study demonstrate that a diet high in dairy products increases the risk of osteoporosis.

In developing your response, discuss the specific evidence needed to support the writer's position.

Facts and Assumptions:

a) Vitamin D and calcium are essential for building and maintaining bones, and dairy products are rich in these substances. The natural assumption is that one must eat these foods to develop and maintain strong bones. Many foods in the plant family are also good sources of calcium and vitamin D.

b) Osteoporosis is linked to both environmental and genetic factors. Did any study participants have genetic markers for osteoporosis? Did any of them live in areas with environmental conditions that could have promoted the development of osteoporosis? These areas could include parts of the world where there are long periods of little sunshine or daylight.

c) A long-term study revealed that participants who consumed dairy products more consistently than other participants suffered more bone fractures. The assumption is that the dairy products contributed to this tendency. It would serve the reader well to know if those participants are ones with genetic markers or who may have lived in the northern latitudes where long, sunny days are few.

d) Bone fractures are symptomatic of osteoporosis. A correlate might be that osteoporosis is the chief cause of bone fractures. Lifestyle is a great contributor to bone fractures. Those who are active and/or risk takers are apt to suffer more fractures than those who live more sedately.

Your notes do not have to be exhaustive. As you begin to write your essay, your brain will generate new ideas. Make certain that you keep the directions in mind as you develop your ideas.

Sample Essay

There is no doubt that sufficient levels of calcium and vitamin D contribute to bone health in humans. Many foods are good sources of these nutrients, but the ones that come most readily to mind are milk and other dairy products. Regular exposure to sunlight is also required to enable the body to synthesize vitamin D. The study cited in this passage suggests that consuming milk and dairy products is detrimental to bone health and may contribute to osteoporosis. The author makes some leaps from the incidence of bone fractures to conclusions about the deleterious effects of milk and dairy products. Assumptions are not sufficient to establish a position. This writer needs evidence to support the argument.

Generalities in the passage need more specificity. A long-term study with a large sample size doesn't tell the reader much. Over how long a period was the study conducted? How many subjects participated in the study? What were the ages and geographic locations of the subjects? These details are important for determining the veracity of the claims in the passage. The passage doesn't even make clear that the study was about the effect of eating dairy products on bone strength. The writer should discover which participants in the study consumed dairy products on a regular basis. If they were young people, it could help to explain the high rate of bone fractures as young people tend to be more active than older subjects. On the other hand, if the sample population was largely made up of senior citizens, their propensities for osteoporosis may result in higher fracture rates.

Assuming that researchers were studying the effects of a diary rich in milk and dairy products, the reader should ask to know how much of each participant's diet consisted of dairy products and which dairy products they were encouraged to consume. Maybe they took to heart the recent campaign that states, "Milk: it does a body good" and drank lots of that beverage. Were their diets replete with cheeses, sour cream, and/or yogurt? The subjects may also have consumed food or drink that has negative effects on calcium absorption. Carbonated beverages have been shown to leach calcium from bones, making them weaker and more susceptible to fractures and osteoporosis. The author cites the fact that developing osteoporosis is linked to either or both genetic and environmental factors. Some subjects in the study may live where pollutants in the air or water affect calcium absorption. Others may live in the northern latitudes where the sunshine necessary for the synthesis of vitamin D is absent for long periods of the year. Some may be genetically destined to develop osteoporosis. Lifestyle changes may postpone the onset of some chronic conditions, but, chances are, if the subjects' parents had osteoporosis, so will they.

Overall, those who conducted this study need to seek and reveal more information about their subjects. The final and, perhaps, most telling statistic is the age of the participants. At the very least, they were considerably younger when the study began than when it ended. Add this to environmental and genetic factors and you have a rationale for the development of osteoporosis, not for the condemnation of milk and dairy products as part of a dietary regime.

Argument Task 29

> *The following appeared in a letter to the editor of a journal on environmental issues.*
>
> *"Over the past year, the Crust Copper Company (CCC) has purchased over 10,000 square miles of land in the tropical nation of West Fredonia. Mining copper on this land will inevitably result in pollution and, since West Fredonia is the home of several endangered animal species, in environmental disaster. But such disasters can be prevented if consumers simply refuse to purchase products that are made with CCC's copper unless the company abandons its mining plans."*
>
> Write a response in which you examine the stated and/or unstated assumptions of the argument. Be sure to explain how the argument depends on these assumptions and what the implications are for the argument if the assumptions prove unwarranted.

Strategies

Argument:

The writer exhorts the readers to boycott Crust Copper Company until the company abandons its mining plans in West Fredonia.

In developing your response, you must identify both the stated and implied assumptions in the argument and explain how the veracity of the assumptions affects the argument.

Facts and Assumptions:

a) CCC has purchased over 10,000 square miles of land in West Fredonia. The writer assumes that, because CCC is a mining company, it will open a mining operation on this land. There is no direct statement in the passage that CCC does have plans for a mine.

b) Mining on this land will cause pollution. Again, there is no evidence in the passage to support this conclusion. Has CCC been guilty of pollution in the past? Even if the company does open a mine, it may have measure in place to abate the pollution that results.

c) West Fredonia is home to several endangered animal species. The writer assumes that any mining activity on the part of CCC will further endanger those species.

d) The environmental disasters can be prevented if the readers boycott CCC products until the company abandons its plans. The assumption that CCC plans to mine on this piece of land is not proven in the passage. There is also the assumption that consumers know which products are made with CCC copper.

Your notes do not have to be exhaustive. As you begin to write your essay, your brain will generate new ideas. Make certain that you keep the directions in mind as you develop your ideas.

Sample Essay

The author of this letter to the editor has used pathos in the hope that the readers will overlook the glaring lack of support for his assumptions. Hot-button words like pollution and endangered species are almost guaranteed to get a desired reaction from the audience. Visions of burning rain forests and dead animals fill their brains, and they are ready to do whatever it takes to stop this destruction and carnage. Although fired up and ready to go, readers must look for the omissions in reasoning created by the author before taking action that could have a catastrophic effect on a mining company.

The author of this letter has chosen his audience carefully by submitting it to a journal on environmental issues. The readers may take his assumptions to be facts. It is a fact that Crust Copper Company has recently purchased over 10,000 square miles of land in the tropical nation of West Fredonia. It is an easy leap from there to assume that the company will open a mining operation at that location. If that eventuality comes to pass, an environmental disaster will ensue. The writer proposes that pollution is inevitable. CCC may have adopted mining practices that reduce or eliminate harmful pollution.

The author also implies that CCC's purchase of land in West Fredonia is an imminent threat to several endangered species that make their home there. This is a large tract of land. If CCC opens a mining operation, it may be nowhere near any endangered animals. It is even possible that CCC has purchased this particular tract of land to establish an animal preserve. The author has purposely left out information that does not serve his intention.

Finally, we have the author' call to action. It is always the goal of persuasion to get the audience to believe in a certain way or to take some action. In this case, the readers are encouraged to boycott goods made with CCC's copper unless the company abandons its mining plans. The problem with this exhortation is the assumption that CCC has plans to mine this tract of land. The other difficulty might be identifying the products that contain the company's copper. It is unlikely that a copper mining company manufactures anything at all. The writer of this letter has provided just enough information to let the readers create their own assumptions about CCC's intentions in West Fredonia.

Argument Task 30

> *The following is part of a memorandum from the president of Humana University.*
>
> *"Last year the number of students who enrolled in online degree programs offered by nearby Omni University increased by 50 percent. During the same year, Omni showed a significant decrease from prior years in expenditures for dormitory and classroom space, most likely because instruction in the online programs takes place via the Internet. In contrast, over the past three years, enrollment at Humana University has failed to grow, and the cost of maintaining buildings has increased along with our budget deficit. To address these problems, Humana University will begin immediately to create and actively promote online degree programs like those at Omni. We predict that instituting these online degree programs will help Humana both increase its total enrollment and solve its budget problems."*
>
> Write a response in which you discuss what questions would need to be answered in order to decide whether the prediction and the argument on which it is based are reasonable. Be sure to explain how the answers to these questions would help to evaluate the prediction.

Strategies

Prediction:

Humana's offering online degree programs will result in increased enrollment and solve its budget programs.

Facts and Assumptions:

a) Omni University had a 50 percent increase in the number of students enrolled in its online programs over last year. The assumption is that this is a large number of students.

b) Omni showed a significant decrease in expenditures for dormitory and classroom space. They don't need dorm and classroom space because instruction takes place via the Internet.

c) Enrollment at Humana University has failed to grow over the past three years. One assumption is that Humana's offerings aren't attractive to prospective students. One might assume that students find Humana too expensive. Humana might have the capacity for no more students.

d) The cost of building maintenance has grown along with its budget deficit. Perhaps the lack of growth has made it difficult for Humana University to meet its maintenance schedule and financial obligations.

Questions:

a) How many students did Omni University have prior to the 50 percent increase? If that number were relatively small, a 50 percent increase isn't impressive.

b) Why were Omni's expenditures for dorms and classrooms so much less than in previous years? The university may have upgraded those facilities a few years ago and have not had to do so in the past few years.

c) Why did Omni begin offering online programs? The school may have been at capacity on campus and began offering online courses to meet the demand.

d) Why has Humana University failed to grow? Its degree programs may not be as relevant as they used to be.

e) Why has the cost of maintaining buildings increased at Humana? These costs may be cyclical. Maybe it has been several years since they have performed significant maintenance on the buildings.

f) What has caused the budget deficit? The cost of doing business has increased while enrollment has remained flat.

g) What evidence does Humana have that online degree programs will increase its enrollment? If Humana's programs were in high demand, its enrollment would not be flat.

h) How will online programs reduce the budget deficit? There are expenses associated with developing online programs. They will need to offer high-demand programs to attract sufficient students to make a dent in the deficit.

Your notes do not have to be exhaustive. As you begin to write your essay, your brain will generate new ideas. Make certain that you keep the directions in mind as you develop your ideas.

Sample Essay

Humana University sees online degree programs as the silver lining in its cloud of financial challenges. The president cites the apparent success of nearby Omni University's foray into that market as justification for his recommendation and prediction. The president would be well- advised to look at some specifics and ask the hard questions before moving forward.

Humana's president should first investigate Omni University's apparent success with its online degree programs. Is a 50 percent increase in enrollment impressive? That depends on the original number of students. If Omni began with 10 students, a 50 percent increase would be 5 students, which is an insufficient number on which to base a new venture. On the other hand, if Omni began with 200 students and increased its enrollment to 300, that would be a rationale for wanting to replicate that success.

Next, the president should ask why Omni University decided to offer online programs in the first place. It may be a case of supply and demand. It may be that more students have demanded Omni programs than the school can meet in its campus location. Online offerings would be a logical solution to that enviable problem. If Humana University hasn't seen that same level of interest in its programs, it may be a prudent move for Humana's president to investigate further before jumping into that market.

Another reason that Humana's president proposes for taking on the challenge of online education is the recent maintenance costs of campus buildings. He assumes that Omni's reduction in those expenses is the reduced need for dormitory and classroom space on its campus. It could just as easily be that Omni completed repairs and maintenance a few years ago and has not needed to repeat them in the last few years. Extensive renovation projects are likely to be cyclical, and Humana finds itself needing to complete those now.

Why has Humana's enrollment remained flat? The school may not be offering programs that reflect current trends in the job market. This, indeed, may be the crux of the problem at Humana. With more high school graduates than ever before going on to some form of higher education, Humana's enrollment should be increasing. Should Humana proceed with plans to offer online degree programs, it may find that students who enroll in those programs will be those who, otherwise, may have come to its campus. Humana may well be left with flat enrollment along with the expense of maintaining its dormitories and classroom buildings. The president's prediction of financial solvency may be a pipe dream.

NOTES

Made in the USA
Middletown, DE
19 January 2021